Living Together Alone

391
65

LIVING TOGETHER ALONE

The New American Monasticism

Charles A. Fracchia

Published in San Francisco by HARPER & ROW
New York, Hagerstown, San Francisco, London

Dedication

I dedicate this book to my children—Laura Elizabeth, Carla Alexandra, Francesca Suzanne, and Charles Anthony—as an expression of my love for them and with the hope that they will always be open to the Holy Spirit and find community in their lives.

LIVING TOGETHER ALONE: The New American Monasticism. Copyright © 1979 by Charles A. Fracchia. All rights reserved. Printed in the United States of America. No part of this book may be used or reproduced in any manner whatsoever without written permission exept in the case of brief quotations embodied in critical articles and reviews. For information address Harper & Row, Publishers, Inc., 10 East 53rd Street, New York, NY 10022. Published simultaneously in Canada by Fitzhenry & Whiteside Limited, Toronto.

FIRST EDITION

Designed by Leigh McLellan

Library of Congress Cataloging in Publication Data

Fracchia, Charles A.   1937—
    Living together alone.

        1.   Religious communities—United States.
2.   Monasticism and religious orders—United States.
I.   Title.
BL632.5.U5F7   291.4   78-3362
ISBN 0-06-063011-6

79   80   81   82   83   10   9   8   7   6   5   4   3   2   1

Table of Contents

Acknowledgments

This book owes a great deal to many people—more than I can conveniently acknowledge. But I must acknowledge the untiring assistance and unfailing encouragement of Sharon Allegra Moore and the warmth and wisdom of Dr. Jacob Needleman, who never failed to share with me his knowledge and insights. Swami Shantananda and Swami Narayan Ananda and all those who generously gave of their time at the Muktananda ashram in Oakland, California; Tessa Bielecki and the eremites of the Spiritual Life Institute in Arizona and Nova Scotia; the Rt. Rev. Vincent Rossi and all those I spoke to at the Holy Order of MANS in San Francisco; Heng Kuan, Heng Shun, and Heng Sure, monks of Gold Mountain Monastery in San Francisco; Abbot David Geraets and the community at Our Lady of Guadalupe Monastery in Pecos, New Mexico; Brothers Philip, Michael, and Jeremy and the community at Christ in the Desert in New Mexico; Abbot Augustine Moore, O.C.S.O., of the Monastery of the Holy Spirit in Conyers, Georgia; Parker Palmer and the community at Pendle Hill in Wallingford, Pennsylvania; the monks at Weston Priory in Vermont; William Irwin Thompson of Lindisfarne in New York; Brother David Steindl-Rast and Father John Giuliani of Benedictine Grange in Connecticut; Father Thomas Keating and Father Basil Pennington and the Cistercian monks at St. Joseph's Abbey in Massachusetts; Father David Knight and Sister Lucy Vinturella of the House of the Lord community in Memphis, Tennessee; Joshua Zim of the Vajradhatu in Boulder, Colorado; Rabbi Zalman M. Schachter of Temple University, Philadelphia; Drs. Richard and Judith Rabkin of New York; Dr. Kevin O. Starr, who encouraged my early researches into the "new monasticism"; and the librarian and staff of the Gleeson Library at the University of San Francisco, who have supplied my needs for books with an unfailing courtesy—all of these I thank most particularly for their time, their generosity, and their encouragement of this project.

Charles A. Fracchia
San Francisco, California
July 31, 1978
Feast of St. Ignatius Loyola

The New
American Monasticism

"WHY are you writing about monasteries?" a friend of mine asked me after I had told him about my work on this book. "They're obsolete. If you want to write about the contemporary religious experience, write about watching football games and crowded shopping centers on Sundays."

His gibing statement compelled me to reflect on my writing project. I had become intimately involved with it, it had consumed almost all of my time for months, and all of my reading had to do with the history of monasticism. I had become intensely interested in the lives of those whom I had met in the spiritual communities I had visited—men and women who exhibited a passion for their way of life, and who, in many cases, had been transformed by their commitments. Had I become too close to the subject? Had I lost a sense of objectivity about the place of monasticism in contemporary life and culture in the United States? Was the "new monasticism," after all, merely a chimerical fad or the experience of a recondite fringe?

This "stepping back" from my project allowed me more perspective. What I saw was a movement of significant importance in contemporary society—a movement that could possibly be one of far-reaching historical importance in the United States. I answered, to my own satisfaction, the query of quantitative importance of the "new monasticism": that it would never involve more than an infinitesimal percentage of the population; that monasticism, even when it has become popular in any given culture, never has included more than a small number of persons. More significantly, I saw the "new monasticism" as providing a leaven in contemporary society that monasticism has not had in Western culture since the Middle Ages.

What is monasticism? What are monasteries? Who are monks? These are questions that we must answer if we are to assess the significance of the "new monasticism"—and to answer for ourselves whether it is truly monasticism. The *Oxford English Dictionary* defines *monastery* as "a place of residence of a community of persons living secluded from the world under religious vows; a monastic establishment. Chiefly, and now almost exclusively, applied to a house for monks; but applicable also to the house of any religious order, male or female." The same dictionary defines *monk* as "a member of a community or brotherhood of men living apart from the world under vows of poverty, chastity, and obedience, according to a rule (characteristic of the particular order), and devoted chiefly to the performance of religious duties and the contemplative life."

What is the popular concept of monks and monasteries? The image of the monk—however gathered—seems to be of someone wearing a distinctive garb, most likely a robe with a hood, who prays and meditates a great deal, is separated from the world in a remote place, is silent much of the time, and is holy or enlightened, or seeking holiness or enlightenment. Such a concept of the monk tallies closely with the dictionary definition; and, most important, it is a good description of traditional monasticism. Oh yes, let us not forget that the word *monk* has been applied exclusively to men.

What is it, then, that constitutes the "new monasticism"? In one way, I use the word *new* in the same sense that it is used in Dr. Jacob Needleman's pioneering book *The New Religions:* not that these religions are new, but that they are achieving new vitality in the United States, and a great deal of attention as religious experiences in this country. Thus, one way in which I use *new* as it applies to monasticism is in terms of the growth in the United States of spiritual communities as a consequence of the spread of Eastern religions.

Another aspect of "newness" in contemporary monasticism is that Roman Catholic monasticism, the principal factor in Western monasticism, is in a period of ferment and transition. Many traditional Catholic monasteries have become open to the spiritual traditions of Buddhism, Hinduism, and Eastern Orthodoxy. And many of these same monasteries are discovering the rich Christian heritage of mysticism and contemplative prayer.

The traditional monastic component of isolation from the world at large has been under scrutiny since the Second Vatican Council ended in late 1965. The ancient conflict in spirituality between "the desert and the city"—a conflict that has resulted historically in the monk and monasticism opting for the desert—is now being reconciled by the conclusion that one can no longer opt for the city *or* the desert. A monk must accept them both, involving himself or herself with the city, but withdrawing in a contemplative spirit in order to know God better.

As yet, the working out of this spiritual dichotomy between "the desert and the city" has not reached any sort of resolution. A few of the Cistercian monks at St. Joseph's Abbey, for example, have taken on as an apostolate the teaching of "centering prayer" to parish priests and to religious in charge of spiritual formation. This monastery, however, continues to consider its "apostolate" to be the contemplative life. The handful of Benedictine monks at the Monastery of Christ in the Desert have chosen a contemplative life in a remote section of New Mexico. To this beautiful desert, however, laypersons and religious both come for varying periods of time to partake in the work and contemplation of these monks.

In their book on an interpretation of Christian spirituality, *The Desert and the City*,[1] the Jesuits Thomas M. Gannon and George W. Traub have written: "Contemporary Christian spirituality must be seen as a continuity between the traditions of the past which it incorporates and transcends and the transcending events of the future. Only with such a perspective can man enter into sacred history and remain open to the renewing action of God in every historical event in the world."

Since Christian spirituality was influenced greatly by the dualism so prevalent in the Roman Empire during the first few

1. Thomas M. Gannon and George W. Traub, *The Desert and the City* (London: Collier-Macmillan, Ltd., 1969), p. 290.

centuries of the Church's existence, and since early theologians —
men such as St. Jerome and St. Augustine — showed themselves so
harshly contemptuous of women, Christian monasticism has
tended to be both separatist and essentially misogynist.

For different reasons, but with the same results, Eastern monasticism has relegated women to a secondary status and has enforced rigorous separation between the communities of men and
the communities of women.

The "new monasticism," however, is developing in a climate of
equal rights for women: not only legally enforced economic,
political, and social rights, but a climate of developing research
into biological, sociological, psychological, and anthropological
factors that tend to promote the androgynous nature of men and
women. And if such androgyny becomes more and more of a
reality in contemporary society, such a new social dimension cannot help having an effect on the theology and on the spirituality of
religious communities.

And so, because there is no etymological reason for not doing
so, my references to *monks* as a generic term will also include
women. I do this rather than categorize men as "monks" and
women as "nuns."

As society's views on women are changing, thus affecting the relationship of men and women in a spiritual community, so are the
attitudes changing towards marriage in a spiritual community. Is
marriage incompatible with the monastic vocation? This is a question that goes to the essence of monasticism, but a question that
probably could not have been asked before now. And would
problems arise if monasteries were open to both men and women?
These are some of the questions with regard to the role of men and
women in the monastic life that are now being discussed. Some
groups have answered them one way, others another way. But
probably at no other time in the history of monasticism have these
questions emerged with such force; and at no other time have
monasteries explored and experimented to provide solutions to
these basic questions in the light of the new consciousness on the
nature of men and women and their relationships. Such questions
are also providing a searchlight into the basic questions of: What
is monasticism? What are its essential components? What is basic
to monasticism and what is peripheral or the result of the cultural
factors prevalent at a certain period?

For much of its contemporary inspiration, the "new monasticism" has begun to review the original sources of monastic inspiration. This has been particularly true of traditional Catholic monastic orders. The Cistercians have been examining the ample literature from the first century of the monastic reform and revival emanating from Citeaux; the Benedictines have been contemplating the unvarnished *Rule* of St. Benedict; and the Camaldolese have been searching for their roots. Never before has there been such an antiquarian revival—and publication—of the written sources for the numerous monastic orders that have arisen during the past fifteen hundred years.

Much of this return to the sources for the various manifestations of monastic spirituality has been positive: the abolition of the distinction between lay brother and choir brother, for example, and the decrease in the clericalization of monastic orders. It has restored a focus, a point of view, to the monastic group, and has stripped away centuries of changes in direction—accretions that resulted from the requests of a pope or prelate for some special work, or the expedient response to some temporal or spiritual challenge. And this return to the sources has rediscovered the dimension of contemplative prayer and mysticism that for so long had been thought to be for only the most exceptional person.

However, the movement of returning to the sources, as commendable as it is, is not the total answer for a renewal of monasticism. The United States in the last quarter of the twentieth century is not the Italy of St. Benedict in the early Middle Ages, or the France of St. Bernard of Clairvaux in the twelfth century, or the Spain of St. John of the Cross in the sixteenth century. What I see developing as one current of the "new monasticism" is not just an examination of and return to the ideals of the past, but a response to present society.

Thomas Merton anticipated this need in the 1960s, when he wrote:

> The first Christian monks went out into the desert not because they believed they were better than other men but because they believed that the Gospel demanded this of them personally: it was their way of interpreting the universal Christian vocation to leave all things, take up their Cross, and follow Christ. This did not imply that others could not fulfill that vocation in numerous other ways. In the Father's house are many mansions. The Body has many members

with different functions. Even within the monastic state there was what we would call a pluralistic choice: one could be a hermit or live in community; one could devote himself to meditation and psalmody or to the service of others; and one could alternate between these and other forms of dedication.

Monastic renewal today is rediscovering this pluralism. While some monks are aware of the paradox that today's "desert" may well be in the inner city ghetto, and therefore go to be tested and to bear witness in the asphalt jungle, others feel it necessary to reaffirm in literal simplicity the primitive desert character of the monastic life. Half a century ago, Charles de Foucauld left his Trappist monastery to live as a hermit in the Sahara, as neighbor and brother to the destitute Tuaregs of the Hoggar. Today the novitiate of the Little Brothers, founded by him, is no longer in the Sahara but in a deserted, canyonlike set of cliff-dwellings in Spain. (It is from here that the Little Brothers go out into the inner city slums or impoverished rural areas.)

Who are the men and women who compose the "new monks"? What are their motivations for this "renunciation of the world"? Is the "new monasticism" a fad or a significant event in contemporary American culture? These are some of the questions to which we must now address ourselves.

Scholars, journalists, sociologists, and others interested in such matters are now debating whether there is a current religious revival, the Third Awakening, in the United States. Some say that the United States has always been a religious country, and that current manifestations of a religious revival exist only because of the searchlight of the media; others believe that the current religious phenomena are signs of a religious reawakening, a heightened religious consciousness, not comparable to what had gone on before because these religious questions have nothing to do with the pollsters' questions of "Do you go to church?" and "Do you believe in God?"

Whether one believes that the United States is experiencing a continued religious movement, now showcased by the media, or whether one sees the current phenomenon as a religious revival, a totally new explosion of religious consciousness, there is no doubt that many aspects of religious life in the United States in the 1970s — and probably the 1980s — are different than they previously were. If nothing else, the current religious movement seems to be ending the many decades of rationalism that marked much of religious as well as secular life in the United States. The failure, so common in academic circles, to take religion seriously as a factor in human lives and in the molding of history, and the implementation of the statement that one "should never discuss politics or religion," seems to be of the past. Religion is becoming more "public"—a factor of everyday life. The current president of the United States, prominent businessmen, students in universities, people in show business—persons from all walks of life are proclaiming their religious faith.

Another manifestation of the current religious movement is the growth of Eastern religions. Even in the 1950s, Alan Watts and others spearheaded acceptance of Zen Buddhism in the United States. But this was a movement limited to a small number of intellectuals, and could best be described as a secular, rather than religious, assimilation of Zen Buddhism.

There is today no wholesale flocking to Eastern religions in the United States, certainly; but the adherents of various forms of Buddhism, Hinduism, and Islam probably number in the hundreds of thousands. Each sect varies, one from another, in its proselytizing, but virtually all groups are conscious of the importance of public exposure.

A burst of evangelical Christianity, among both Protestants and Catholics, is yet another consequence of this new religious consciousness. This has been most pronounced among Roman Catholics, for whom the evisceration of the institutional vitality of the Church and the confusion and transitional pain of the period after the Second Vatican Council have meant totally new directions of spirituality.

Out of this new religious consciousness has come a revival of interest in separating oneself from the world, becoming a member of a spiritual community, and seeking greater spiritual perfection. It is this phenomenon that goes by the general name of "monasticism." Monasticism can be traced back 5,000 years in Hinduism, 2,000 years in Buddhism, and 1,700 years in Christianity. It seems to be a correlative function of religious movements. And in most religious movements, monasticism provided the sinew, the cause of reform and purification, the ideal of the religious experience at various times.

What is happening in the United States today is a significant revival of both Western and Eastern monasticism in their "pure," or historic, forms, as well as the development of new forms of monasticism.

Although sociological studies of the "new monks" are, as yet, lacking, there have been sufficient studies, coupled with my own observations, to allow me to make some general statements about those men and women entering spiritual communities: they are white, middle-class, in their twenties and thirties; many of them are products of the countercultural revolution of the 1960s and 1970s. They were politically radical, questioning the material values of their parents, and seeking altered states of consciousness through drugs, unconvinced of the doctrine of self-fulfillment through successful careers or higher education.

There is a similarity between these young men and women of today and the thousands who, during the third and fourth centuries A.D., fled the sensuous and civilized urban centers of Egypt, Syria, and Palestine for the desert. Experimenting during the freedom of the 1960s and 1970s, and exposed to a broad array of luxuries of the consumer economy, these young men and women have eschewed drugs and multiple sex experience and have turned their backs on color television, suburban ranch-style homes, the "get ahead" mentality, sports cars, and digital watches.

They also have turned away from social and political activism. It was as if an entire generation had "burned out" in trying to make "the world a better place to live in." The end of the war in Vietnam and the loss of energy in "the great society" signaled an end to activism—but not to the aspirations of this generation. Many of them asked, "Is that all there is? There must be more." And many of them discovered this "more" in religion and in spiritual communities.

Society periodically goes through anti-intellectual times; and, since the United States had harnessed the intellectualism of the universities and colleges to serve the technological and industrial complex, when one's degrees no longer led to jobs and studies didn't seem to have any relevance to one's life or aspirations, education became yet another source of disillusion.

The generation that demonstrated for peace had little trouble adjusting to the concept of interior peace that could be found in a spiritual community; the generation that had been sated with material goods found little problem in renouncing material possessions; and the generation that saw "the best and the brightest" involve the nation in a disreputable war and prove incapable of solving basic problems of human need turned away from the traditional goals of their parents and sought answers in a transcendent way.

The religious backgrounds of the "new monks" are diverse, but as yet no comprehensive study has been made of what the percentages are from the various faiths. Again, without statistics, but from my own observations, I was surprised to discover the large number of men and women from Jewish backgrounds who had become members of spiritual communities of Eastern religions. Some had come from religious families, but most were from nonreligious, secular backgrounds.

It is difficult to speculate about the reasons for this phenomenon. Are the causes to be found in the generations of effort toward Jewish assimilation in the United States that reduced religion to occasional, formal, almost social observances? And does the lack of this religious, transcendent background now create a desire among Jews for some religious experience? Or are Jews in their twenties and thirties seeking a more positive affirmation of Judaism through the vehicle of the Eastern religious experience in the United States?

There are certainly Jews to be found in Christian spiritual communities; but by far the large majority gravitate to Buddhist or Hindu spiritual communities. This, of course, has a social and historical basis: the almost two thousand years of warfare and antipathy between Christian and Jews were unknown in Asia.

Both Rabbi Zalman M. Schachter of Temple University and Dr. Jacob Neusner of Brown University have written on Jewish spiritual communities.Rabbi Schachter very specifically set out the plan for a Jewish spiritual community in an article entitled "Toward an Order of 'B'Nai Or': A Program for a Jewish Liturgical Brotherhood."[2] In recent correspondence, Rabbi Schachter informed me that he expected such a community to begin some-

---

2. Zalman M. Schachter, "Toward an Order of 'B'Nai Or'; A Program for a Jewish Liturgical Brotherhood," in *Contemporary Judaic Fellowship in Theory and Practice* ed. Jacob Neusner (New York: Ktav Publishing House, 1972).

time soon. The fact remains, however, that a large number of Jews have gravitated to Eastern spiritual communities.

Yet another large constituent religious group in the spiritual communities of Eastern religions is that of Roman Catholics. The appearance of Roman Catholics in Eastern and non-Catholic Christian spiritual communities is one of the most surprising features of the contemporary new religious consciousness and of the "new monasticism." Roman Catholicism is numerically the largest religious group in the United States. Generations of religious ghetto-living has, within the last two decades, given way to an ecumenical spirit and to assimilation within the mainstream of American life. Roman Catholicism probably has the largest complex of monastic groups of any religion in the world. Why, then, are increasing numbers of young Roman Catholics turning to other religious experiences and to the spiritual communities of other religious groups?

The spirit of change that struck Roman Catholicism after the Second Vatican Council coincided with the political, social, and psychological upheaval that gripped the United States at that time. The changes—both religious and secular—that this volcanic period wrought created turbulence throughout the country; but probably no single group was more affected than U.S. Roman Catholics.

These changes brought confusion—and then indifference. The U.S. hierarchy and clergy responded to the Second Vatican Council and to the social upheaval about them by vague attempts at accommodation and what they called "bringing the Church into the modern world." The ancient mysteries and beauty of the Roman Catholic liturgy gave way to an overly verbal mass. Parishes provided little sense of community and did little or nothing to inculcate a sense of prayer among those who continued to partake in Catholic worship. Bishops continued to issue their "pronunciamentos" to the laity; but there were fewer and fewer persons who listened or cared. The institutional vitality of the Roman Catholic Church was dead—a death that John Kenneth Galbraith has called the greatest social displacement he has observed in his lifetime.

While the official Church was wondering what to do about what seemed to be mass apostasy (even though *apostasy* seems to be too active a word for Catholics lapsing into indifference), and while it proliferated folk masses to "get the young people to come back to the Church," Eastern and Christian spiritual masters and teachers were gathering around them the young men and women I have described above. Most of these masters and teachers taught a return to the traditional religious concepts: to a rigorous morality in the face of a now-exhausted "sexual revolution"; to an elaborate liturgical worship; to a system and structure of faith that had been deemed antiquated by most institutional churches, including Roman Catholicism.

While pastors wrung their hands about empty churches and continued pallid liturgies, young Catholics were chanting Sanskrit praises to the Baba Muktananda amidst rich symbolism that Catholicism had just given up. While Catholic doctrine seemed to be in a limbo, the venerable Master Hsuan Hua was commenting on the interminable sutras. And while bishops concerned themselves with bureaucratic details and administrative tasks, Christian and Eastern religious teachers were teaching thousands how to meditate.

There are other factors involved in this drift of Catholics to Eastern and to other Christian spiritual communities. While Catholicism developed brilliant theologians, capable administrators, and individuals of great sanctity, it did not develop the spiritual master and teacher. This may be because of the centralized, authoritarian structure of the Church. Or it may be due to the fear, latent in Catholicism, of seeming to entrust the operation of God's grace through the vehicle of some individual who, through his wisdom and knowledge and through his personal qualities of spirituality, may pass on his or her insights and qualities of life to another.

Another factor in this Roman Catholic moribundity is rigidity. Except for the Catholic charismatic renewal, the only movement in U.S. Roman Catholicism at this time that has any vitality, there has been no development of flexible institutions for Catholic spiritual communities. Whether this is because of their history of canonical paternalism or because years of dependence on familiar established institutions have atrophied imaginative leadership in the Church, it is difficult to say.

Even though the wholesale departure of Catholic priests and

religious from their vocations in the 1960s and 1970s now appears to be over, Catholic men and women have been entering seminaries for the diocesan clergy, monasteries, and novitiates of religious orders in much fewer numbers in recent years. (The exception might be the numbers entering Catholic contemplative orders.) That decreasing numbers of Catholics are opting for a life in Catholic spiritual communities at a time when persons are entering other such communities at an unprecedented rate can only mean that Catholicism in the United States has not yet perceived the necessity for new approaches to the monastic life.

As one former Catholic, a young woman who had become a member of a Buddhist spiritual community, said to me: "I was born and raised a Catholic, and I have a good feeling about the Church. But when I was in college, and I was searching for some spiritual meaning for my life, I couldn't find it in Catholicism. Maybe it was there; but I looked, and couldn't find it."

Protestants, too, have flocked to the "new monasticism." Like secular American Jews, many U.S. Protestants have had only a vague religious experience. The liberalizing tendencies in U.S. Protestantism established churches that were virtually denuded of liturgy and the sacraments, bereft of symbolism, and devoid of contemplative prayer. And, as with the Jews, Protestants have virtually no monastic tradition. The Anglican monastic communities and the community of Taize have not attracted any large numbers of Protestants seeking life in a spiritual community.

Those of a Protestant background have principally joined Eastern spiritual communities and new Christian communities—from the Unification Church of the Reverend Moon to the Holy Order of MANS.

The Eastern Orthodox monasteries, the richness of Orthodox spirituality, and its mystical liturgy have not yet been discovered by westerners. This may be because of the nationalism that has been so prevalent in the Orthodox churches and the association of Eastern Orthodoxy in the United States with an aging population of immigrants.

William Irwin Thompson, founder of the Lindisfarne community in New York, claims that the current appeal of spiritual communities to men and women in their twenties and thirties is due to unresolved parental conflicts on the part of these young men and women. This view, I must say, I find overly skeptical. Although the irresolution of one's relationships with one's parents is certainly a major factor in the desire of many to escape to a familylike, or family-substituting, spiritual community, I do not believe that the "new monasticism" can be attributed to such a simple basic cause.

However, Thompson does provide a clue to the primary reason for the contemporary popularity of both Christian and Eastern spiritual communities in the word *parents*. The word triggers a mental response of *family*—and then of *community*. It has become a cliché that westerners have lost a sense of community and that the nuclear family, increasing urbanization, and the anonymity of the technological state have all contributed to the decline of community.

In the past, religion frequently has provided a bond cementing the concept of community. This was true of the Jewish tribes' covenant with Yahweh. And it was true of those "societies of friends"—the small communities of men and women who had accepted Christianity—that dotted the shores of the Mediterranean, tied together by visiting teachers, communicating with each other by letter, and sharing the excitement of their faith. The small towns of New England, centered around the now picturesque church, are yet another example of these religiously inspired communities.

It can be argued that Christian monasticism began as the result of a seeking for this ideal of a covenant community—a recreation of those early Christian "societies of friends." And it can be argued that the "new monasticism" is an aspect of this age-old search.

I was struck—at each spiritual community that I visited—by this sense of community, and by the manifestations of forging a sense of community. "This is my family," one monk told me. "I came here [from a Catholic contemplative monastery that stresses solitude] because I wanted a sense of community, others to help me in pursuing my vocation," a young Benedictine monk said to me. "I look upon my fellow monks as my brothers," a young man in a Buddhist monastery confided to me, "the bhiksunis [Buddhist nuns] as my sisters, and the venerable Master as both father and mother."

The search for spiritual community is nothing new in the life of the United States. Small groups of religious dissenters settled this country. The nineteenth century saw the country dotted with religious communes and spiritual utopias. But the search for community today—as exemplified by the "new monasticism"—seems to have intensified. As the nineteenth-century utopians reacted to the spreading of a corrosive industrialism, so do today's communitarians seek escape from a technological and industrial landscape from which spiritual values have been driven.

Even the nuclear family has exploded: a rampaging divorce rate has helped mightily to create the fifty million unmarried adults in the United States—and to add to the desperate search for community.

It appears that the spiritual community is only the first of the community types that will emerge. Social and economic needs will produce others. Communities based on common interests, literary and artistic as well as religious, will bring others into being—perhaps like the communities in England that centered around Nicholas Ferrar in the seventeenth century and Eric Gill in the twentieth century.

The escape from the dehumanizing aspects of urban alienation and the trackless wastes of suburban anonymity began in the 1960s as an almost romantic movement of "back to the soil." The future, I believe, will see communities seek roots in the concrete of the cities and the suburbs.

Communities can also center around defiance or exclusivity. One of the binding ties of the early Christian "societies of friends" must have been the ever-present threat of martyrdom. The thrill of being an initiate in a small sect, feeling different as a result from the rest of the world, privy to some gnostic knowledge, can be a potent force in one's adherence to a spiritual community.

This would certainly be a negative aspect in the search for community that characterizes the "new monasticism"; but one cannot deny that it exists. "You should join us," one young man said to me, his eyes sparkling with his "in" knowledge of his group's teachings and lifestyle, "and your eyes would be opened . . . would they be opened!"

In addition to the search for community, another major aspect of the "new monasticism" is what I choose to call the *affective* in religious experience—or the revolt of the heart against the head.

In the terms of Christianity, particularly Roman Catholicism, this experience (thought by some to be the result of the Second Vatican Council) seems to signal the end of the scholastic domination of the Christian message, and a return to a Biblical and patristic vision—in short, a knowledge of Christ and a life of virtue being correlative, feeding one another, one not outstripping the other.

There is an analogy here in the Eastern experience as well: the Buddhist teaching that meditation helps people to respond to "what is really there," the use of chanting in Hinduism to catch the energy of the universe and make us one with it, the Buddhist suspicion of thoughts and words, and so forth.

What I believe is important in this element of the "new monasticism" is not the nuances of doctrinal development or the intricacies of the Buddhist or Hindu visions of the cosmos, but a conscious attempt by those who participate in the "new monasticism" to live the life of their religious convictions as the logical conclusion of belief. This is not to imply that monasticism previously presented a dichotomy between belief and how one lived one's life; but it does mean a change of attitude—a closer adhesion between the concepts believed and the life lived. Such an attitude is illustrated by those in spiritual communities who have said to me, "Come, live our lives, participate in what we are doing." There has been no call to theological discussions or doctrinal workshops.

This second aspect of the "new monasticism" is allied to a third aspect: the importance of the teaching figure, the divine incarnation. The result of the revolution of Descartes in the seventeenth century was eighteenth-century rationalism; and this rationalism has had continuing effects to our own day. It has stripped the divine from religious experience, and consequently caused ritual and symbolism in religion to be looked upon as embarrassing relics of superstition. Religious leaders such as Jesus and Buddha were reduced to liberal reformers. Thus, for today's rationalist, the new religious consciousness, particularly as witnessed in the "new monasticism," is a wonder: a significant turning away from deistical abstraction to a sense of immediacy, personalness, and ritual celebration of the divine.

The derision that greeted the recitation of the rosary during my boyhood, a derision based upon the "stupidity" of such repetition, seems humorous today as increasing numbers of Catholics twist their Jesus Prayer beads, Hindus clutch their beads while repeating mantras, and Buddhists repeat the name of the Buddha countless times, accompanied by numerous prostrations.

The tendency in Christianity to abstract Jesus Christ by the use of such words as *Christ*, or *God*, or *the Lord* is countered by the charismatics' talk of "Jesus" as a present reality in their lives, and their calling out to him during prayer meetings as if he were an existing "lover."

The words of the scriptures—the gospels, the vedas, the sutras—are not looked upon as charming fairy tales, but are literally interpreted, seen as personally directed to oneself, looked upon as containing the essence of life.

For the skeptic, these aspects of the "new monasticism" evoke puzzled looks, the feeling that this represents a retrogression. How can a Harvard graduate with a brilliant career ahead of him become a Buddhist monk? How can an attorney who was involved in founding one of the most prestigious public advocacy firms in the country live in an ashram? How can a brilliant Radcliffe graduate live in a Catholic charismatic monastery? Who can believe in "hungry ghosts" and "speaking in tongues"? And why get up before 4 A.M. to chant the Divine Office in a Benedictine or Cistercian monastery, or the praises of the Buddha in the Tathagata Monastery?

There can be little response to these queries. The era of apologetic controversy seems to be over. Instead, there is only an invitation to observe, to partake—an invitation that increasing numbers are accepting.

The skeptic will also have other questions about the effectiveness or the use of the "new monasticism"—as skeptics always have questioned the utilitarian nature of the person who separates himself or herself from the world. In the case of the "new monasticism," it is not always the flight to the desert that involves such separation, but a flight from those values that our society holds sacred. And it is towards subverting these values—the paganism of the post-Christian era—that both the revival of Christian monasticism and neo-Oriental monasticism will have its effect.

In each of the monastic communities I visited, no matter how remote, I was struck by the numbers of persons who came to visit, to look around, to talk with the monks—persons drawn not just by curiosity, but by some greater force—perhaps a desire to find some peace, tranquility, and harmony in their lives. And, once more, the message is present: Here in the monasteries are persons who choose to be poor. They eat to sustain life, they clothe themselves to keep from nakedness and to indicate their withdrawal from the world, and they don't need to numb themselves with television or to expand their energy in disco dancing. And yet they have something that many of us don't have—they are happy.

Is it realistic to say that an infinitesimal number of monks are going to make this difference in our society? Is it merely a utopian pipe dream that more than a minuscule percentage of the population will ever be changed by the witness of the "new monasticism"? Will any change be confined to the recondite few?

It is always perilous to prophesy a major change in society's values. However, I believe that the phenomenon we have been describing—the "new monasticism"—is itself the outcome of the spiritual malaise that grips the United States, of an emptiness that cannot be filled.

Related to the expected effect of the "new monasticism" on the consumerist values of the United States are its effects on jobs and the attitude towards money. The men and women I interviewed in spiritual communities throughout the United States—particularly those who worked at outside jobs—all gave their jobs their best; but in most cases their jobs were only vehicles to support their minimal needs.

"I work in a health food store three months each year," said one man who lives in the Muktananda ashram in Oakland, California, "and that gives me just enough money to sustain myself. I don't need any more."

A young woman with a Ph.D. in English literature from a prestigious Ivy League university is a resident in a spiritual community and works part-time as a waitress in a restaurant. Another, with a Ph.D. in Oriental languages, works in a boutique. Both indicate that their jobs, which they perform scrupulously, only serve the necessary purpose of supporting themselves.

"My entire life is centered in this community," one of them told me, "and every moment that I have is spent here. But in our life each one of us has to contribute to the support of the community—

rent, food, things like that—and that means I have to work two or three days a week. Why should I have to work any more? To buy things that I don't want or need? To save? If everyone worked for just his or her needs, you'd wipe out unemployment."

It isn't only that jobs have become simply vehicles for elementary sustenance: the "new monasticism" has also begun to change attitudes about how one views those jobs.

"One of the reasons for my conversion and for my coming to live in this community," a middle-aged member of one spiritual community related to me, "was that I finally realized the insanity of my life. I had spent years in 'getting ahead' in my job; and, as I advanced through promotions, I still wasn't happy. And then I looked at what it had cost me: a divorce, estrangement from my children, bouts of high blood pressure and ulcers, consumption with a lot of negative thoughts and feelings about people whom I thought were after my job or about persons whose jobs I wanted. Well, it finally dawned on me that this kind of life didn't make any sense. In an attempt to find out what did make sense in life, I became a member of this community. And I even solved my job situation. I couldn't afford to quit working because of my obligations to my ex-wife and children. But I saw a position with my company doing work I enjoyed, and decided to ask the president for it. It meant a drop in pay and a lowering in status. The president and the board thought I was crazy—but that was fine with me."

Such attitudes towards jobs on the part of the "new monks" do not mean that this work is sloppily or mindlessly done, however. "I give my job the same importance I give meditation," one member of a spiritual community said to me. "All things in the world are sacred," said another, "and if you're going to do something, like work at a job, even if it's one that you don't like, you've got to see it as a liturgical act . . . it's part of worship."

The owner of a company who employed several members of a nearby spiritual community on a part-time basis revealed to me: "If I could, I'd staff my entire company with them. They're just tremendous: they produce almost twice the average, they don't gossip or quarrel, they follow orders without any back talk. I realize that they're not working here because they're ambitious to get ahead or anything like that, but I've never seen anyone who puts such concentrated effort into their work."

And, in the midst of this technological-industrial state, many of these monastic groups are breathing new life into cottage industries. The baked goods of the Tassajara Bakery, an operation of San Francisco's Zen Center, are nationally famous. The baking of bread is also a major enterprise at the Cistercian Monastery of the Holy Spirit in Conyers, Georgia. Gourmet preserves are produced in another Cistercian monastery—that of St. Joseph's Abbey in Spencer, Massachusetts. The weaving of ponchos, rugs, wall hangings, and liturgical vestments helps to support Christ in the Desert.

A tendency towards the production of quality food—such as the Tassajara baked goods—and towards the production of both aesthetic and practical goods that emphasize quality design and workmanship marks the growing cottage industries of the "new monasticism."

Intimately related to this concept of jobs, work, and money is the concern for environment. Taking as little as possible from the environment is a corollary of the philosophy of working to sustain oneself.

The development of monastic communities during recent years has tended to use existing facilities. Gold Mountain Monastery converted an unused warehouse. At the City of Ten Thousand Buddhas, the facilities of an abandoned state hospital have been used. The harmonious blending of the adobe buildings at Christ in the Desert with the landscape of the high desert country of New Mexico is an architectural accomplishment of the most sensitive proportions. And the monks of the Spiritual Life Institute in Nova Scotia are planning a reforestation project on their wilderness land to replace the scraggly growth that has resulted from the property having been timbered crudely in the past.

Another area where the "new monasticism" provides witness for a new way of life is in relationships. As with money and the environment, the United States as a culture has developed the exploitation of other human beings to a fine art. People are used and tossed aside with the same abandon as electrical gadgets and automobiles. *Love* has become so bankrupt a word that many persons are embarrassed to use it. Relationships are frequently nothing more than one party extracting a desired goal from the other—or perhaps each using the other. The inability to form lasting and significant relationships is probably the principal malaise of our time.

Jim Steele, in his mid-twenties and a member of the Catholic charismatic community at the Benedictine monastery of Our Lady of Guadalupe in Pecos, New Mexico, gave me a clue to the insight of the "new monasticism" into relationships. Each member of the Pecos community is encouraged to have a prayer partner and, because the community believes very strongly in the enhancing complementariness of men and women, most of these prayer teams consist of a man and a woman.

"It's not only that we pray together each day," Jim told me one day while we sat on a lawn in front of the monastery, "but we become very close to each other—like brother and sister—sharing each other's thoughts and feelings, ministering to each other. We are celibate, but we love one another. You know, I think this is a great preparation for marriage."

He was not implying that celibacy should be a factor in marriage, but he was saying that this level of relationship, this dimension of nurturing another person, and of being nurtured by that person, provides an element in a relationship that is often missing—that that person is loved for himself or herself and not for something that he or she can provide at that moment or sometime in the future.

Monks historically have had a reputation for eschewing people. Their only relationship, it is said, is with God; their only preoccupation, the quest for spiritual perfection; and their only path, that which, when followed, purifies them to partake of the divine. But monastic spirituality is seen more and more to be involved with others: the role of the monk who scurries away from "the world" and lives a life of total self-involvement is seen as a narcissistic one.

What is it, then, that the "new monasticism" has to teach us about relationships? It is perhaps the sanctity of other humans as the basis of a relationship. The analogy to things may not be too far-fetched: we should not pollute the air or the water, we should not destroy fish or animals needlessly, we should not deplete the fertility of the soil, we should not proliferate ugliness in nature. Why? Because creation is sacred. And if the land, the sea, and the air around us are sacred—and if we diminish ourselves by consuming more than we need, by damaging the environment—how much more do we lessen our humanity by using other human beings for our gratification? It is this paradoxical lesson of attachment through detachment that the "new monasticism" offers our society.

Is it realistic to assume that the revival of interest in monasticism, bringing with it values of sanity for the contemporary world, will bring about any significant change in our society? Or will the "new monasticism" be but a false hope, yet another chapter in man's historic optimism that utopian religious communities can change the world? And will the witness of the "new monasticism" with regard to relationships change the views of the predators in singles bars from San Francisco's Union Street to New York's Second Avenue? Will the petrochemical companies look upon the monastic movement as having anything to say to them about the environment, or will the motivation of maximum profits continue to predominate?

At the risk of ridicule for being a visionary, I believe that the "new monasticism" will provide a catalyst for change, will be a conscience for the nation, will change the values of many with regard to work and money, relationships, and the environment. I see the "new monasticism" as institutionalizing the ferment of the 1960s and 1970s: the consciousness of nonviolence, the ecological movement, the desire for relationships that see the essence of each encountering the other, the wish for a contemplative life. In this institutionalization will come, hopefully, a source of vitalizing our society, of holding forth the possibility of a life that is both sane and full.

In many ways, the "new monasticism"—both that of the East as well as that of the West—resembles the monasticism of Western Europe during the Middle Ages: where a structure grew out of the spiritual witness of the community, integrating the religious and spiritual needs of the monastic community with the needs of the surrounding society. Whereas many Christian monasteries in Europe and the United States tended to become indistinguishable from the mendicant and active orders in that the monastery became a house for a religious apostolate—much the same being true in the Far East—the emphasis today is on the individual spiritual life of the monk. The outreach of the monastery emanates from this fundamental principle.

All the monastic groups have programs that give information

about their communities and the religious backgrounds of the communities. Many have the capability of having individuals come to stay for a period of time for their own spiritual refreshment. Some allow those who are not members of the community to participate in community life for varying periods of time. Even the sale of the products of monastic cottage industries is oriented towards the justifiable end of helping to support the community and of providing goods of both utility and beauty.

On the other hand, the individual alone as a monk was how Christian monasticism began; and the phenomenon of the monk who wished to pursue his or her own spiritual vision was very much a continuing tradition in Eastern Orthodoxy. The enlightened master in Oriental religions frequently chooses to be alone.

The current experience in the United States, nevertheless, is that of disaffection with one's previous spiritual community combined with a vague idea about a different approach to monasticism. Most people have discovered that there are few St. Benedicts, Trungpa Rinpoches, or Hsuan Huas: men who are not only spiritual leaders, but who have the charismatic qualities, vision, and organizational abilities to begin a new spiritual community.

But I see a continued growth of the "new monasticism," a continued influx of those joining these communities, and a steady increase in the number of monasteries. This development, I believe, is as much due to the current search for community as it is due to the aspect of religious conversion. Whatever the reasons, spiritual communities will continue to be a magnet for an increasing number of persons.

Such spiritual communities offer one a community in which to share religious growth as well as a fundamental communitarian spirit. They serve as places where one can shed his or her former life and begin anew, where one can learn to pray or meditate or chant—and from whence he or she can emerge, with a spiritual commitment, to take one's place in the world.

And it is in the form of temporary communities that the future of the monastic experience will witness perhaps its greatest growth and see the greatest impact on society. Imagine, if you will, a modern city dweller, subway-riding, cafeteria-eating, overdressed, under-read, working on an assembly line, punching time clocks, forever caught up in a rat race, surrounded by gadgets, and institutionalized to an absurdity. Can such an individual share the monastic experience? He (or she) not only can, but he must. And can he have this experience without going off to some remote spot for the rest of his life, vowing celibacy, and devoting every moment of his days to specific spiritual practices? Most assuredly he can.

The explanation is that monasticism should not be understood in historical specifics and development. The religious leaders of the world meant that each life should be molded around their teachings, rather than being an imitation of their lives. When one of these leaders—say Christ or the Buddha—taught the values of an interior, meditative life, he meant these values to apply to throngs on city streets, not merely to solitaries in forests or deserts. When we are commanded to love one another, this injunction applies to our neighbors in the inner city of New York, the suburbs of Chicago, and the rice paddies of Vietnam, not just to the other members of a monastic community.

It is our consciousness of these teachings—of Christ, of the Buddha—that counts, not a memorization of the circumstances of their lives that gave rise to their teachings. It is the living of our own lives that matters, not the repetition of their lives. Consciousness, then, is an awareness of our duty to our lives.

Such a consciousness begets a conscience. Once a man or woman is made aware of the sacred nature of living, of the sacred possibilities of life, then he or she is forever committed, must be completely devoted, to the spiritual life. Indeed, the life of their very souls is bound to this life.

This, I believe, is the essence of the "new monasticism": a recognition of its many possibilities for the resacralization of the lives, not just of the few who elect to live according to the historical tenets of monasticism, but of the many more who must work to support themselves, who wish to marry, and who live in houses and apartments in New York and San Francisco, Seattle and Miami, and on farms in Kansas, Oregon, and Georgia.

It is appropriate that I discuss the basis for my selection of the spiritual communities about which I have written here. I was interested in presenting a range of monastic possibilities in these pages and in recording the changes and ferment in the monastic ideal. Despite those who challenge the fact that a religious revival has been going on in the United States during the past decade, it is my opinion that the contrary viewpoint is quibbling. Out of the religious revival has come a monastic revival as increasing numbers are seeking to live their lives—or some portion of them—in a religious community.

By no means is this book a comprehensive directory of monastic groups in the United States. I have written about two Buddhist groups and one Hindu group to illustrate the varying forms of Eastern spiritual communities; but I did not write about Sufi communities or about San Francisco's Zen Center, which a number of spiritual leaders consider to be one of the foremost monastic communities in the United States.

The decision not to include some spiritual communities was not based on any premise more infallible than considerations of time and space—and whether the community was sufficiently representative of the range of experience in the "new monasticism" that I wished to convey.

In so far as possible, I have made few or no judgments on the monastic communities. Instead, I have let these communities tell their own stories, unfold their own experience.

2

The New Trappists
St. Joseph's Abbey

THE massive stone buildings of the monastery thrust onto the
rural New England landscape like some medieval anomaly—a
Hollywood set for an epic. Set among some twelve hundred acres
of farmland and woods, the Cistercian monastery of St. Joseph's
Abbey in Spencer, Massachusetts, is one of the oldest monastic
communities in the New World, tracing its lineage to monks
driven from France at the time of the French Revolution. After
several moves, the abbey was located in Spencer in the early
1950s. The Cistercian monks (known popularly as Trappists)
transformed the existing farm buildings for their community
needs and began to build the church and other buildings on the
model of famed medieval Cistercian architecture—massive, un-
adorned, practical.

The Cistercian Order stems from one of those periodic reforms
of Benedictine monasticism—this one in A.D. 1098, when a group
of monks founded a monastery at Citeaux in France for the
purpose of retaining the purity of the primitive spirit of St. Benedict. Within a short time, there were Cistercian monasteries
throughout Europe; and it became one of the most widespread religious orders in the Middle Ages.

The word *Trappist* has become almost synonymous with the concept of austerity in monastic orders—a concept widely disseminated by the popular writings of the Cistercian monk Thomas Merton. In the past, Trappist monks eschewed meat and dairy products; they never spoke, unless absolutely necessary, using instead a well-developed sign language for occasional communication; they slept very little; and their lives were devoted to prayer and work.

It is paradoxical, therefore, that this monastic order, known for its conservative religious way of life and for its search for seclusion and a life of contemplation, should become one of the most vital forces in the contemporary United States for Catholic spiritual renewal.

It is late when I emerge from a taxi hailed at nearby Worcester. A full moon silhouettes the tall tower of the abbey church and makes the snow glisten with a soft whiteness. I trudge towards a building that a sign proclaims as the guest house, and am met at the door by two monks: the genial, white-haired Brother Paul, who is the guest master, and Father Basil Pennington, tall, bearded, and looking like a Hebrew prophet. They wear the traditional black-and-white robes (called a "habit" in the parlance of religious orders) of the Cistercian order.

The two men conduct me to a sparsely furnished but pleasant room in the guest quadrangle, which is part of the monastic complex centering around the abbey church. I unpack rapidly and am led down a long corridor to the guest dining room, where I am given supper. We chat for a while after I have eaten in the oak-paneled dining room, and Father Basil tells me that the Cistercian order has changed considerably during the past decade, following the re-examination of monastic life after the Second Vatican Council. The different status between choir monks and work monks was abolished. There was some relaxation in the rigid rules concerning diet, sleep, and conversation. Heads are no longer shaved in a broad tonsure. And the sources of Cistercian spirituality are being examined as a vehicle for monastic renewal.

I return to my room after our conversation and finish unpacking before going to sleep. The next morning I am awakened at 6:15 A.M. by Brother Paul knocking on my door. I rise, hurriedly shave, brush my teeth, shower, and dress. The guest master leads me through the labyrinthian corridors of the monastery, and we enter the large church.

The monks of St. Joseph's Abbey are entering through another door and are filing into the choir stalls that flank both sides of the church. At precisely 6:45 A.M., the sound of sixty voices chanting Lauds, the morning prayer of the Divine Office, fills the church. With the exception that the prayers are now chanted in English, the ancient Gregorian chant still prevails. Three cantors step to a lectern situated in the main aisle of the church and intone the beginnings of the psalms for the prayer of that day. The assembled monks chant the responses—the ageless prayer of Christian monasticism, with its roots in the very early days of monastic development. The church is filled with the clear, cadenced rhythms of the chant: "Glory be to the Father, the Son, and the Holy Spirit." Each monk makes a profound bow towards the center, where the Blessed Sacrament is kept, behind the altar. "Come, let us bow down in worship; Let us kneel before the Lord who made us. For he is our God, and we are the people he shepherds, the flock he guides."

The chanting of Lauds lasts for about thirty minutes, and at its conclusion several of the monks who are priests leave their choir stalls to vest for the eucharistic liturgy that will follow.

Approximately ten priests concelebrate mass. A short, bald monk plays the tracter organ that accompanies the monks as they chant the liturgy. "The mass is over. Go in peace"—and the monks leave their stalls and file out of the church to begin the day's work.

I walk through the cloisters and the rooms through which I had come, and find myself back in the guest quarters, where I go to the dining room for breakfast. This time there are about twenty men there, awaiting their morning meal. These are the retreatants who come from throughout the eastern states each weekend for three days of prayer, silence, and talks on the spiritual life. So popular are these retreats that each weekend is "booked" several months in advance.

Father Basil enters the dining room as I am finishing my ample breakfast. We walk through the large monastic complex and view the extensive cloisters—built in the same style and pattern in which Cistercian monasteries have been constructed for almost a thousand years. The combination of stone walls, dark wood paneling, and tile floors evokes a sense of austere beauty; and the restrained furnishings are in keeping with the practicality and dignity of the architecture.

The tour takes me to the monastery's two libraries, to the monks' refectory with its long rows of dark wooden tables and stools, through the kitchen, to the chapter room, and into the monks' living quarters. Father Basil tells me that private rooms for the monks are a recent innovation, that formerly the monks all slept in a dormitory. The small rooms are furnished with a bed, a desk, and a chair. Each monk has some different decorative feature in his room: one has several plants, another a small Byzantine shrine, yet another some framed pictures of saints.

The monks at St. Joseph's Abbey sing the liturgical hours as monks have done for centuries — except that today they are sung in English.

The church and cloisters are built as a quadrangle around a large courtyard, which we now cross to visit some of the outlying buildings. In these buildings the monks perform the work that is not only an essential part of the Cistercian religious life, but that is also the principal source of income for the abbey.

First, we visit the operation of Trappist Preserves, the preparation of fruits for the gourmet jams and jellies that the abbey produces. Huge vats and the whirring of an assembly line with jars being filled seem strangely out of keeping with the tranquility of the cloister from which we have come. Several monks are working silently at the various tasks: truckloads of fruit become preserves that then fill the countless jars that come spinning down a conveyor belt.

A loud clanging bell announces that another batch is ready, and the monks spring to their places—ready to process more jars of jams and jellies.

Trappist monastic rules insist that a monk must never remain idle, even under the pretext of contemplation. He should earn his living by his work; but, as St. Jerome insisted, the monk works with his hands not only to earn a living, but above all for the good of his soul.

Our next stop is a building in which the Holy Rood Guild—the name for the operation that makes ecclesiastical vestures—is located. St. Joseph's Abbey is one of the largest sources of custom-made church vestments in the United States; and we tour the operation to see the different aspects of production: the large bolts of cloth, the cutting and sewing—even the pen where a number of sheep (whose wool is used in making of vestments) are peacefully munching hay.

The monks engaged in the design and manufacture of vestments silently and efficiently bustle about, carrying out their duties. The place could have been located in New York's garment district.

As we make our way back to the cloister, a tractor rumbles by us—a reminder that the anticipated arrival of spring will spark the revival of the monastery's extensive farming operations.

Father Basil leads me to a visitors' parlor, where I am to meet the abbot of St. Joseph's Abbey, Father Thomas Keating. A tall, spare man enters the room and greets me with a warm smile.

We discuss the changes that have swept through the Cistercian order during the past decade and how these changes have affected St. Joseph's Abbey.

"You must understand that every Cistercian abbey is different," Father Thomas begins. "We are not a centralized order. Every abbey is jurisdictionally independent—even though we have an abbot general and meet periodically in a general chapter with representatives from each monastery attending. So I can only speak for what is happening at St. Joseph's.

"Vatican II caused a revolution in monastic life. We were forced to re-examine our lives as monks to determine what our roles should be in modern society — what was essential to our monastic vocations and what practices were accretions acquired over the past few centuries in response to different conditions from those which exist today.

"Out of this re-examination came many of the changes that you've probaby already witnessed. The hours spent chanting the Divine Office have been cut down, and it is now chanted in English. The rules on silence have been relaxed somewhat. The difference between the choir monks and the work monks has been abolished: now all monks both work and chant the office.

"I think that perhaps the rigidity which has crept into the Cistercian way of life during the past few centuries — a rigidity which characterized much of what had happened in the Church since the Reformation — has been exorcised, and we are returning to the rule as it was formulated when the order was founded."

The abbot's intensity and precision are indicative of the monastery itself. The community of some sixty monks ranges in age from one monk in his nineties to monks in their twenties; and the response to change and to new concepts of spirituality has not been wholehearted enthusiasm among the monks of St. Joseph's Abbey. However, Father Thomas's approach has been quite successful: a blending of the traditional Western Christian spirituality with an openness to both Eastern (or Orthodox) Christian spirituality and the religious and spiritual concepts of the Far East. It is a blend that has worked well at St. Joseph's Abbey.

We are joined by Father Joseph Chu-Cong, a Vietnamese who is master of novices at St. Joseph's Abbey. It is coincidental that a Far Easterner happens to be in charge of the spiritual formation of the young monks at a time when experimentation with incorporating Hindu and Buddhist spiritual practices in Christian — or, more precisely, Cistercian — spirituality has become a factor at St. Joseph's Abbey; but the coincidence is providential at a time when many Catholic spiritual leaders are discussing contemplation and mysticism as central in importance in the spiritual life of the Church.

I ask Father Joseph about those who are entering St. Joseph's Abbey to become Cistercian monks, and he replies that 95 percent of those entering the abbey do so after college, that they are mostly from the eastern states, and that most of them are from Catholic backgrounds. The monastery receives more than two hundred applications each year for admittance as observers; but, after careful screening, only a small fraction of that number are admitted.

These are admitted as observers for two months, and then they are sent away to reflect and decide whether they are called to the life of a Cistercian monk. If this decision is affirmative, the candidates return to spend six months as postulants. At the end of this time they become novices for two years, after they take their first vows. Another four years of training takes place, and then final vows are taken.

Training will vary among the dozen or so that enter St. Joseph's Abbey each year. There is a basic spiritual training that is common to all monks; but some will study for the priesthood, in which cases academic and theological studies will be intensified.

Father Joseph, following the lead of Father Thomas, has opened the abbey—particularly the younger monks—to incorporating Zen and other Eastern spiritual practices within their own spiritual lives.

"A number of the monks use Christian koans, for example," Father Joseph tells me, "and utilize Zen to gain insight into the Christian truth. For instance, here are a couple of Christian koans: 'How do you realize God when you make the Sign of the Cross?' and 'How do you realize yourself when you make the Sign of the Cross?'

"About a dozen monks sit zazen each day for at least two hours, and maybe about another dozen utilize transcendental meditation practice. And I guess about a dozen more practice hatha yoga.

"The experience has been most positive. It hasn't been that we try these Eastern spiritual practices only because they're fashionable today, but because they are excellent methods for developing our life of prayer and for bringing us closer to God."

The assimilation of Eastern spiritual practices into the spiritual life of St. Joseph's Abbey is not limited to their use by a minority of the monks there, Father Thomas tells me. Eastern spiritual leaders have come to the monastery, lectured, conducted workshops, and witnessed the contemplative and mystical spirit of Christianity. In the late spring of 1977, Father Basil helped organize and participated in a conference held in the rural community of nearby Petersham, Massachusetts, where some forty monks, nuns, and laypersons from both the East and the West met to study ways in which Western, Christian monastic communities could "open up" to the heritage of Eastern religions, such as Buddhism and Hinduism.

In the process, the Petersham meeting laid the theoretical groundwork for an historical development in monastic life that would see it more actively involved in the transformation of the world.

According to the report issued by the symposium, "the problem of our encounter with other religious traditions should be seen in the wider context of the transformation of particular cultures into a world culture. Monastic life should thus find the expression of its values and religious experiences in the contemporary world without losing its roots. . . . Monasteries should be in the front line of this work of creation."

And in a final address, one of the conveners of the Petersham symposium, Abbot Cornelius Tholens, O.S.B., from Holland, called for a "mystical revolution . . . in which mankind becomes aware of the deep religious meaning of existence. Monks by profession, and men and women who discover the monk in themselves, have to assume a great responsibility in this movement. Far from considering this mystic way of life an escape from history and the world, as many do, we know that meditation and prayer are in the center of reality. . . . Our human way is to become more conscious of total reality in its depth and height, in its worldly and divine dimension. In this sense mystics are much more realistic than those locked in a one-dimensional world."

"The symposium grew out of a movement inspired by the Second Vatican Council document on non-Christian religions, which recognized—and encouraged—the plurality of means in the journey of the soul," Father Thomas says. "The effort to meet and assimilate Eastern religiousness was made through the vehicle of monasticism because the monastic life is the form of Christian life closest and easiest to understand for Eastern religions. Among the Christians, monks seem to be the best-suited persons for the dialogue with them and for introducing the East into a knowledge of Christianity."

There is a knock on the door. Brother Paul announces that the midday meal will soon be served. Father Thomas and Father Joseph depart for the monastery's refectory, where the only communal meal of the day is eaten in silence. The monks have already gathered twice—at mid-morning and before lunch—in small groups to recite the hours of Tierce and Sext of the day's office. Following this midday meal, they will rest or perhaps take a walk until 2 P.M., when they will recite None, another of the hours of the office, and spend the remainder of the afternoon working, reading Scripture, and studying.

I follow Brother Paul to the retreatants' dining room, where I have lunch. Once more, as I am finishing my meal, Father Basil comes in. We walk together through the monastery and talk about St. Joseph's Abbey's active role in attempting to bridge the spiritual worlds of the East and the West.

"Father Thomas saw the benefits being derived in our community from contact with yoga, Zen, and transcendental meditation, like the facility they offered the young and the not-so-young to enter into a deeper life, and encouraged the monks here to go deeper into their own contemplative heritage and, also, to seek more simple and practical ways of sharing these, which they have found in the Centering Prayer movement which I'll talk about with you later," Father Basil tells me.

"But, for others, the route will be different. Many in the West will never be open to the perception of the values of the meditative traditions of the East until they first go deeply into their own tradition.

"This seems to be more the route followed by Thomas Merton. In spite of his very cosmopolitan background, his early vision as a Cistercian was circumscribed. But as he grew in contemplative depth, he opened out to become the great seer of our times. I have spoken to some of the Eastern masters who met Father Merton on his last journey. They have said that no one from the West has understood them so well. Yet, scholars examining the Eastern writings of Merton find his knowledge not that extensive. Rather, he, from the depths of his Cistercian experience, typical Western Christian mysticism, met these masters in the depths of their experience, and they knew they were being understood."

We walk into the library with its high-vaulted ceilings, its dark polished wood set against the brown tile floor, and long refectory tables, where some monks are reading, and we sit near a window that overlooks the large courtyard.

"Work and pray" enjoined St. Benedict, founder of Western monasticism. A Trappist monk works making liturgical vestments.

"A couple of years ago I had occasion to visit a Ramakrishna temple in Chicago," Father Basil says, "and I talked to a number of the disciples, all from Christian backgrounds, who had gathered around the swami there. When I asked them what had drawn them to the temple, they answered that they could find no one in their own churches who was willing to lead them into the deeper ways of the spirit where they could truly experience God.

"And even among priests and religious I have talked to, I have found that they have felt it presumptuous to seek the various stages of contemplative prayer—even though in most cases they have been taught methods of prayer and meditation.

"What this led me to see is that Christians today believe that contemplative prayer is something only for the rare few. As a result, we have developed a method of opening out to this contemplative prayer by a technique which we call 'centering prayer.' St. Joseph's Abbey has undertaken to encourage the teaching of this method throughout the country."

Father Basil describes the technique—drawn from Cistercian monastic practices, and found expressed in a fourteenth-century mystical treatise called *The Cloud of Unknowing*. The technique is based upon centuries of Christian mystical tradition, and yet sounds uncomplicated.

"First," Father Basil continues, "at the beginning of the prayer we take a minute or two to quiet down and then move in faith to God dwelling in our depths; and at the end of the prayer we take several minutes to come out, mentally praying the 'Our Father.'

"Then, after resting a bit in the center in faith-full love, we take up a single, simple word that expresses this response and begin to let it repeat itself within.

"And finally, whenever in the course of the prayer we become aware of anything else, we simply gently return to the Presence by means of the prayer word. That's all there is to it."

Such a simple technique has long disappeared from the spiritual life of Christianity, as Father Basil points out, but is central to the Christian contemplative tradition. And its rediscovery in Christianity today is what the Cistercian monks of St. Joseph's Abbey are seeking.

The evening rays of the winter sun slant through the windows of the library, and the bells of the abbey church announce that vespers is about to begin. We leave the library and walk through the long, spacious cloisters towards the church. I am struck at how sparkling clean everything appears.

I take my place in the back of the church and watch the monks enter in the gathering darkness of the early evening. There is silence; and then the chorus of some sixty voices begins the chanting of the church's evening prayer:

> Happy is the people that knows well
> the shout of praise, that lives, Lord,

in the smile of Thy protection . . .
What else but Thy glory inspires
their strength?

The monks go off to a light supper after vespers is concluded, and I return to the retreatants' dining room for dinner. Depending on the evening, these Cistercians will have a period of leisure, a class, or a conference before going to chant the final prayer of the day—Compline—at 7:40 P.M.

Only two candles, burning on the altar, serve for light in the church during Compline. In this darkness the monks conclude by chanting the "Salve Regina, Mater Misericordiae," and then file out of the church. As each leaves, Father Thomas sprinkles him with holy water, giving a blessing. The traditional role of the abbot, as spiritual father, master, and teacher is evident in this solemn, moving ritual.

The monks go off to bed—for they must rise at 3:15 A.M. for an hour of vigil in the church from 3:30 to 4:30, followed by personal prayer, Scripture reading, and a light breakfast before the chanting of Lauds at 6:45 A.M.

As I leave the church, I walk past a stone fountain, carved in the Middle Ages, which used to grace a now-forgotten Cistercian monastery. Father Basil had explained to me that these fountains were prescribed by Cistercian rules to be placed outside of the monastery's refectory for the monks to wash their hands before eating. The fountain at St. Joseph's stands now as a decorative reminder of a medieval concern for hygiene.

So much has happened to the Cistercians since that fountain was carved! Marco Polo had not yet journeyed to China; and the European voyages of exploration of the fifteenth, sixteenth, and seventeenth centuries were yet a long way off. And here in a rural New England setting, in buildings that duplicated medieval Cistercian architecture, were monks who continued to follow a daily schedule of work and prayer that their predecessors had formulated almost a thousand years before, and who were attempting to enrich Christian spirituality both by an assimilation of Eastern spiritual practices and by a rediscovery of their own rich contemplative tradition.

3

The Buddhist Orthodoxy of Gold Mountain Monastery

S OMEWHERE on U.S. Highway 101, which follows the eighteenth-century Spanish trail of colonization, Heng Sure is on a bowing pilgrimage. He set out in 1976 from the Ch'an Buddhist Gold Wheel Temple in Los Angeles and plans to arrive at the Sino-American Buddhist Association's "City of Ten Thousand Buddhas" —the Buddhist monastery near Ukiah in northern California— sometime in 1979. Heng Sure's pilgrimage consists of taking three steps, and bowing in a full prostration . . . taking three more steps, and bowing in a full prostration . . . for the approximately seven hundred miles of his journey.

At the City of Ten Thousand Buddhas, a former state hospital that has been purchased by the Sino-American Buddhist Association for a monastery and center of Buddhist studies, the venerable Master Hsuan Hua releases a score of turtles in a stream on the occasion of Buddha's birthday—a ceremony known as the "liberation of life," when animals destined to be slaughtered are purchased and released.

At the Gold Mountain Monastery in San Francisco, a novice monk, Sramanera Kuo Chi, has constructed a boxlike chair to train himself to sleep sitting up.

What seems to be a religious lifestyle that one reads about and believes takes place only in the exotic Far East has become established in the United States; and about thirty men and women have chosen the rigorous life of a Ch'an Buddhist monk or nun. Many others have become followers of the venerable Master Hsuan Hua but have not elected to become monks.

This remarkable adherence to the Buddhist path in the United States began in 1962, with the arrival in San Francisco of the Master Hsuan Hua, the ninth patriarch of the Wei-yang lineage in China. In 1968, an explanation of the Surangama Sutra by the Master Hsuan Hua, which lasted for ninety-six days, led to five persons there becoming Buddhist monks and nuns—the beginning of what is today a growing and thriving monastic community.

Running contrary to the tendency to westernize and sanitize Eastern religious movements in their appearance in the United States, the Sino-American Buddhist Association, founded by the Master Hsuan Hua, has retained the age-old teachings, customs, and way of life of Ch'an Buddhism. Men and women live separately; most eat only one vegetarian meal each day; the Chinese language of the Buddhist scriptures is retained (even though an extensive translation project has been under way); and chanting, meditation, and ascetical practices are retained as they have been traditionally handed down.

I ring the doorbell of a converted three-story red brick building in San Francisco's Mission District, and I am let in by two monks. This is Gold Mountain Dhyana Monastery. A tiny entry hall contains some of the publications of the Sino-American Buddhist Association; and twin glass doors lead from this room into a large room with a very high ceiling. This is the Buddha Hall or, as it is called by the monks, the Jewelled Hall of the Great Heroes. In front of a large shrine of the Buddha, located at one end of the hall, are offerings of flowers and fruit. A lecture platform and table are also situated here: for the readings of and the commentaries on the sutras. Rows of kneeling cushions and a chair, reserved for the Master Hsuan Hua, are placed in the middle of the hall and comprise the only furniture in the room. There is a shrine to Kuan Yin Bodhisattva in the back of the hall, and paintings and photographs of Buddhist saints and patriarchs hang on the walls.

I have arrived shortly before 11 A.M., and Heng Kuan and Heng Shun, the two monks who have greeted me at the door, invite me to partake in the midday meal. This is the only meal that the monks eat each day, and according to Buddhist precept it must be eaten before noon. I am led into yet another long room with rows of wooden tables and wooden stools. At one end of the room there is a table upon which are set bowls and pots containing the vegetarian dishes for the meal.

Members of San Francisco's Gold Mountain Monastery listen to the translation of the Buddhist sutras from Chinese to English. A monk (with earphones) provides the translation.

The monks have gathered in the Buddha Hall, and I join them there, where the ritual known as "the high meal offering" is taking place. Incense is lighted before the shrine of Buddha, and the monks recite a litany of the names of Buddhas and Bodhisattvas, chant mantras, and take food from the altar and feed "the hungry ghosts." After a succession of bows, the monks file into the dining room, where more verses are recited to the accompaniment of the ringing of a small bell.

I follow the monks after this ceremony and fill my bowl with the savory-smelling food, take some tea, and sit at one of the long tables. The meal is eaten in silence as the monks contemplate during this time. At the conclusion of the meal, the monks once more file into the Buddha Hall, chanting the name of Shakyamuni Buddha.

When this ceremony is finished, Heng Kuan and Heng Shun take me to the guest room on the second floor of the monastery. The two young monks are clothed in the traditional grey robes, brown outer garments, and sandals of the Buddhist monks. Their heads are shaved.

Heng Shun, born Gregory Wilczak in 1951, grew up on the West Side of Chicago. The profile of Heng Shun in one of Gold Mountain's publications states: "High on his list of favorite pastimes were lying, stealing, drinking, and fighting. Gregory got so involved in this destructive lifestyle that he ignored his studies and failed every subject in his high school sophomore year."

It is difficult to imagine this quiet, withdrawn man as the same person described in the journal. Following a period in a military academy, Heng Shun reverted, says the biography, to his former ways. Somehow, his life changed; and after a growing interest in Eastern religions, he went to Bangkok, where he lived in a monastery. As the result of reading the biography of the Master Hsuan Hua, Heng Shun decided that he would follow him.

"With a single reading," Heng Shun relates, "I knew the Master was my teacher, the feeling was that strong. I had never recognized anyone as my teacher before; and being conceited, I thought I didn't need one. But after reading about this master, I faced the East and bowed to him one thousand times in the morning and one thousand times in the evening for four days straight. In June of 1974, I took off my monk's robes, bought a plane ticket to San Francisco, and changed my diet to eat only vegetarian food. I arrived at Gold Mountain, but only stayed a week for the first time. To truly cultivate the Way as people do here is not an easy matter and, frankly, I was caught off-balance, chickened out, and ran home."

But two months later he returned, and on July 24, 1975, Gregory Wilczak became Heng Shun, a novice at Gold Mountain Monastery. In August, 1976, he became a bhikshu, a fully ordained monk.

A far different life was lived by Heng Kuan, born near Boston in 1943. Heng Kuan was the model schoolboy, excelling in sports and studies. His career at Harvard, where he graduated with honors in

English literature (his senior thesis was entitled "Illusory Life-Death Cycles in Eugene O'Neill's Plays"), was equally distinguished.

Shortly after graduation he accepted a commission as an officer in the U.S. Navy, married, and was assigned to duty in Taipei, Taiwan. A growing dissatisfaction with his military experience led him to study Buddhism; and in 1968, although he had never encountered him, the young naval lieutenant began to contemplate becoming a disciple of the Master Hsuan Hua. This he accomplished in 1969, when he returned to the United States. A fortuitous release from his commission as a naval officer and an amicable divorce allowed Heng Kuan to follow the Buddhist path more intensely. While doing so he received a Mirrielees Fellowship in poetry to write at Stanford for two years, leading to a master's degree. The following year, however, Heng Kuan returned to Taiwan, this time as a Buddhist novice, a disciple of the Master Hsuan Hua, to become invested as a monk.

A gong sounds: it is noon — time for the repentance ceremony. Heng Shun and Heng Kuan depart for the Buddha Hall. This ceremony begins with an offering to the Buddha; then, as the monks complete some one hundred prostrations, there is homage paid to the Buddhas and Bodhisattvas, and the monks recall their offenses and repent of them. Finally, the "Great Compassion Mantra" is recited twenty-one times.

The repentance ceremony takes one hour, and at its conclusion the monks sit cross-legged and meditate for the next hour.

I take the opportunity to read a book entitled *With One Heart, Bowing to the City of 10,000 Buddhas*. This book contains the journal of Heng Sure, a monk whom I had met a few years earlier and who is now on a bowing pilgrimage from Los Angeles to Ukiah. The book tells about his thoughts and what has been happening to him and his companion during this time.

Heng Sure, I remember, had just become a monk at Gold Mountain when I first met him. He was a Midwesterner who had studied at Middlebury College in Vermont, majoring in Chinese, and then transferred to Oakland University in Michigan, where he graduated *cum laude*. Then he proceeded on to the University of California at Berkeley as a Danforth Fellow to pursue graduate studies in Oriental languages. There he received his master's degree. Heng Sure had been born Christopher Clowery in 1949, and during his studies at Oakland University and at Berkeley he became interested in Buddhism. This interest ripened during a trip to the Far East.

In a biographical sketch, Heng Sure wrote of his decision to become a monk:

Even then I was constantly plagued by doubts of my future, how to harmonize and blend all the things I wanted to do, astrology, photography, theater, music, writing, teaching, etc., all forms of communication, when the underlying message is missing. The voices nagged incessantly until May of 1974, when I entered Gold Mountain Monastery for a week of retreat and thesis work. Miraculously, suddenly, the inner voices fell silent for the first time in four years. I rejoiced in the silence and decided to walk through the opening door that approached. The only remaining choice is no choice at all—leave home, become a bhiksu [monk], obediently and diligently apply the Master's teachings to my own life, support the Triple Jewel, and help bring the medicine of the Buddha-dharma to the unwell patient America, Canada, and the West.

It is difficult to imagine this scholar of Oriental languages, cheerful Buddhist monk, and articulate expounder of Buddhism spending two years traversing nearly the length of California, subjecting himself to the elements, the fatigue of walking and bowing, the harshness of concrete and asphalt, and the ridicule and hostility of many who come upon the sight of him walking three steps and prostrating himself along the highways of California.

Heng Shun quietly interrupts my reveries. The hour of meditation is over: it is time for the sutra lecture, he tells me. This quiet, almost self-effacing monk has made a vow not to eat more than one bowl of food each day, and to take no food or drink other than water after the noon hour, until daybreak the next day. Despite the austerities of his ascetical life, I notice no "spiritual pride" about him, no haggard look of the self-conscious ascetic.

The sutras are the Buddhist scriptures. Many of these have not been translated, and each day a portion of one of these sutras is read in Chinese, translated, and then commented upon. The reading, translating, and expounding of the sutras is not only for the enlightenment of the monks at Gold Mountain Monastery, but also for wider dissemination.

"The Sino-American Buddhist Association is dedicated to

bringing the genuine Buddha-dharma to the entire world," Heng Shun explains to me. "Because language is a vital tool in the communication of these teachings, one of the Association's most important objectives is the accurate translation of the Buddhist canon into English and other major languages of the Western world. This is essential if Buddhism is to become truly assimilated into the culture of the West and yet maintain the principles set down by Sakyamuni Buddha. The Buddhist Text Translation Society was formed for just that purpose."

A Buddhist nun at the City of Ten Thousand Buddhas contemplates after eating her midday meal.

The sutra is read from the lecture platform in front of the Buddha shrine in the Buddha Hall. A portion is read in Chinese, and then the reader stops while an earphone-bedecked translator, sitting to the right of the reader, gives the English translation while listening to the tape of what has just been read.

This reading in Chinese, translating into English, commentary in Chinese, and translating of the commentary into English goes on with alternating rhythm until 3:30 P.M., when the monks will once again spend an hour in meditation.

I stay for a bit in the Buddha Hall. The late afternoon sun is shining through two large windows, highlighting the bright red, gold, and green colors in which the shrines are painted. A stillness pervades the hall. The monks sit motionless on their meditation cushions.

Ch'an Buddhism, developed in China, was transmitted to Japan, where it is known as Zen Buddhism. Unlike Zen Buddhism, certainly as expounded in the United States, Ch'an Buddhism, as expounded by Ch'an Master Hsuan Hua and practiced at the Gold Mountain Monastery and at the City of 10,000 Buddhas, is replete with a vast, syncretistic mythology. Gods and goddesses, ghosts, and good and evil spirits are all part of the Buddhist religious cosmology.

If there is one characteristic that marks the Ch'an school, it is silence. D. T. Suzuki discusses this in his *Essays in Zen Buddhism:*

> At the time of the introduction of Zen [Ch'an] into China, most of the Buddhists were addicted to the discussion of highly metaphysical questions, or satisfied with the mere observing of the ethical precepts laid down by the Buddha or with the leading of a lethargic life entirely absorbed in the contemplation of the evanescence of things worldly. They all missed apprehending the great fact of life itself, which flows altogether outside of these vain exercises of the intellect or of the imagination. Bodhidharma and his successors recognized this pitiful state of affairs. Hence their proclamation of "The Four Great Statements" of Zen. . . . In a word, they mean that Zen has its own way of pointing to the nature of one's own being, and that when this is done one attains to Buddhahood, in which all the contradictions and disturbances caused by the intellect are entirely harmonized in a unity of higher order.

Ceremony and ritual—along with chanting and meditation—are yet another aspect of Gold Mountain Monastery's search for enlightenment. Heng Shun, for example, not only spends time each day studying the *Avatamsaka Sutra*, known as "the king of sutras," but he also spends two hours each day bowing to the *Avatamsaka Sutra*.

What seems so at variance with contemporary society in the United States—and, in reality, in the Far East today, also—is accepted by the monks at Gold Mountain Monastery with enthusiasm as the ordinary scheme of things for monks. In fact, many will go beyond the basic requirements for living as monks to take vows that expand their asceticism: Heng Sure's bowing pilgrimage is one example; Heng Shun's eating only one bowl of food each day is another. Some monks take vows never to touch money; others vow complete silence for long periods of time; still others vow not to own any possessions except their monks' robes and a few sutras.

I wander up to the second and third floors of Gold Mountain Monastery. The rooms for monks, residents, and visitors are on these two floors—small cells, almost barren of furniture and decoration. These rooms are used by the monks for work and study, but rarely to sleep in. (Most of the monks at Gold Mountain Monastery sleep sitting up in the Buddha Hall.) Individuals who are interested in Ch'an Buddhism may stay at the monastery. Although not required to adhere to the same schedule as the monks, these residents must observe certain rules of the monastery, maintain the Five Precepts (which prohibit killing, stealing, sexual misconduct, lying and harsh speech, and consumption of intoxicants), and partake of some of Gold Mountain's spiritual practices.

Meanwhile, in the Buddha Hall, meditation has given way to an hour of language lessons, as the monks learn Chinese, Sanskrit, and other languages. Those already proficient in the sacred languages of Buddhism work at translating the sutras for the Monastery's extensive publishing program. (In variations of the schedule at Gold Mountain, the times from 8:30 to 10:30 A.M. and from 1:30 to 3:30 P.M. are used for work, including translation.)

Another hour of meditation takes place from 5:30 to 6:30 P.M., followed by the evening recitation and the sutra lecture. The evening ends with the chanting of a mantra—the first twenty-seven lines of a mantra from the *Shurangama Sutra*. The mantra is repeated forty-nine times as the monks walk the perimeter of the Buddha Hall.

The schedule at the Monastery calls for lights out at 10 P.M.

However, this seems to have little meaning for the monks, most of whom sit in the Buddha Hall and meditate. As the hours go by, these solitary figures, still in the flickering light of candles, drop off to sleep. Most have trained themselves to sleep sitting up; and when they awaken during the night, they continue to meditate until sleep overcomes them again.

Alternately dozing, awakening, meditating, and falling asleep again, the monks at Gold Mountain Monastery spend the night sitting on meditation cushions in the Buddha Hall. At 3:30 A.M., a tattoo beaten on two boards and the ringing of bells will summon them to begin a new day.

My return to 3636 Washington Street in Pacific Heights, San Francisco's elegant residential district, was filled with nostalgic memories. I had lived in this twenty-two-room brick mansion with my wife and family during the last two years of my marriage. When I purchased the house in the late 1960s, I had hoped that I would live there for the rest of my life. That was not to be.

As I walked up the white marble steps to the entrance, I smiled at the coincidence that this house is now the setting for a convent of Buddhist nuns and the International Institute for the Translation of Buddhist Texts.

A pretty, dark-haired young woman opens the door. She introduces herself as Kuo Tsan—born Terry Epstein. The house was as I remembered it: the great oak staircase leading from the large foyer to the second floor; the two parlors, one an exquisite room done in the style of eighteenth-century France, the other a large room with rosewood paneling; the dining room with its spectacular view of the Presidio, the Golden Gate Bridge, and San Francisco Bay. . . .

It was as I remembered it, but there were differences: in the front parlor there was now a shrine to the Buddha; in the rosewood-paneled living room there was the headquarters for the International Institute for the Translation of Buddhist Texts; the dining room continued its original function, but the rooms on the top two floors, formerly bedrooms and a study, were now occupied by several "bhiksunis"—Buddhist nuns.

Wearing grey robes and with their heads shaven, the lives of these Buddhist nuns resemble those of the monks across the city at Gold Mountain Monastery: the schedule is the same, the spiritual practices are the same, and both spiritual communities follow the venerable Master Hsuan Hua.

Kuo Tsan introduces me to a stern-appearing young nun. This is Dharma Master Heng Yin, who serves as the leader of this community and who is an accomplished translator of the sacred Buddhist Scriptures from Chinese into English. Born in 1946 in Seattle, Heng Yin studied philosophy and Oriental languages at the University of Washington. After graduating, she had thought about entering a Catholic contemplative order. "However," says Heng Yin, "I realized that Western religions had not discovered a method for release from the transitory world of forms."

She worked briefly in the peace movement but became dissatisfied with "dealing with the symptoms and not the cause of suffering." Heng Yin had become interested in Buddhism while at the University of Washington, and began to believe that the answers for which she searched might be contained in the Buddha-dharma. She heard of the Master Hsuan Hua and traveled to San Francisco to meet him. Attending first an intense seven-day meditation session and then a ninety-six-day summer session of meditation and study of the *Shurangama Sutra* in 1968, Heng Yin decided to become a Buddhist nun, which she did in mid-1969.

Kuo Tsan leads me to the bottom floor of the building. This area had once served as a ballroom for the house. What were supplementary servants' quarters are also on this floor. The entire floor has now been transformed into an elementary school, of which Kuo Tsan is the principal.

The school serves the small children of the women who reside at the Washington Street convent and Institute as well as children of persons not affiliated with the Sino-American Buddhist Association.

We go upstairs, where those nuns and laywomen who are working on the translation of the Buddhist sutras are hard at work. The paraphernalia of the translator—dictionaries, lexicons, grammars—are much in evidence. Each translator has tape recorders and earphones. The tapes contain the commentary of the Master Hsuan Hua on the sutras; and the commentary is included in the published text.

A small child of one of the laywomen resident in the convent toddles by. She is probably not yet three. I look at her and smile—and remember when my own children walked and played on these same parquet floors.

Arriving in Ukiah, I ask directions to the City of Ten Thousand Buddhas. A gas station attendant with a bemused look on his face tells me to follow the road I am on. In a few minutes I reach the former state hospital, which is now owned by the Sino-American Buddhist Association.

All of the hospital buildings—of which there are more than sixty—and 237 acres of land were acquired by the Association for what is fast becoming a center for religious, educational, and social programs for world Buddhism.

It is early evening when I arrive. The birds are chirruping and the wind rustles the pine trees, but I do not see anyone as I walk along the streets amidst the complex of buildings. Finally, as I pass a building that was the gymnasium of the old hospital, I hear an amplified voice.

The door to the gymnasium (now called Kuan Yin Hall of Ten Thousand Buddhas) is open, and I walk in. About fifty persons are sitting on cushions on the floor at small desks. In front of them, seated at a table, is the Tripitaka Master Hsuan Hua. Dressed in saffron and scarlet robes, the Master is speaking in Chinese. It is the time for the reading and commenting on the sutras. The Master completes his talk and sits patiently while a young woman wearing earphones over her shaved head, seated on a platform at the venerable Master's right, fiddles with the tape recorder. She then translates into English the commentary given by the Master Hsuan Hua. When she finishes, the Master reads another passage from the sutra, gives a commentary, and stops. The young woman gives a translation.

I sit in the back of Kuan Yin Hall for the next hour, listening to the rhythmical reading of the sutra and to its translation. Abruptly, the Master completes his commentary, rises, and leaves the stage. The young woman translates, and soon she, too, finishes.

Sramanera Kuo Yu, a novice monk at the City of Ten Thousand Buddhas, introduces himself to me and invites me to partake in the evening recitation. He hands me a booklet that contains the transliteration of the 27-line mantra from the *Shurangama Sutra*, and I join the file of Buddhist monks, nuns, and laypersons as they walk around the room chanting to the beat of a small, melodious bell.

My mind swarms with ideas as I chant the mantra, having no sense of its meaning, during the first few times walking around

Kuan Yin Hall. Then, the "inner chatter" stops, and I feel quietly content and peaceful.

Forty-nine times we walk around the gymnasium; and forty-nine times we recite the 27-line mantra.

The bell stops ringing, and each of us goes to a meditation cushion. The ceremony of bowing to the patriarchs now takes place; and when it is over, Sramanera Kuo Yu takes me down the street, across a courtyard, to an empty two-story building.

"We've made up a bed for you here," he informs me.

The room is high and narrow. There is no furniture except for the bed. A bright light shines overhead.

I find that I can't fall asleep, and read for a bit. I finally sleep—only to be awakened at 3:30 A.M., when there is a knock on my door. The monks are now awakening at the Tathagata Monastery, which is adjacent to the building in which I am sleeping.

I put on my clothes, wash in a bathroom down the corridor, and then walk outside to locate the monastery building in the blackness of the night. It takes me a few moments to find the large hall where the monks have gathered for the morning recitation, and I arrive just as they are beginning to chant the Leng Yen mantra.

Around me is the evidence that the monks have not had to travel far to come to this Buddha Hall, reminiscent of the one at Gold Mountain Monastery: the blankets that they had wrapped themselves in during the night are folded on the floor next to their meditation cushions.

The morning recitation lasts for an hour. Before the meditation period that follows, the monks are given a tea break. Heng Lai comes up to me, introduces himself, and offers to direct me to the dining room.

One corner of the cavernous dining hall is illuminated by a light. I sit at a table while Heng Lai goes to the kitchen to obtain some tea, and when he returns he joins me at the table.

Heng Lai was born Eric Weber in 1946 to a Catholic family, and spent a year during high school in a Franciscan seminary. After he graduated from high school, Heng Lai joined the navy, and, when his stint was completed, went to work on a salmon fishing boat and then as a seaman for an oceanographic institute.

"It was while I was on a six-and-a-half-month cruise of the Mediterranean that I had this unusual experience," Heng Lai tells me. "While I was sitting on deck, my thinking went wild as if in a whirlwind towards some unknown point. I couldn't control it, nor did I want to, because it was somehow right. Then there was silence and an incredible feeling of peace. This was followed by a feeling of aliveness and nowness that lasted about a week. I was determined to find out what this feeling was."

Shortly after this experience, Heng Lai left the oceanographic vessel and went to San Francisco. He attended a sutra lecture and later a three-month study and meditation session at Gold Mountain Monastery, felt a strong attraction to the Master Hsuan Hua and to Buddhism, and sought to become a disciple. The Master accepted him; but when Heng Lai was told that he must become a Buddha as the result of this discipleship, he mistrusted his ability to live such a life and left for a year.

Heng Lai returned in 1971, become a novice, and then a monk.

It is dawn when I leave Heng Lai and walk back to the building where I had slept. The day is the celebration of Buddha's birthday, and already visitors are arriving at the City of Ten Thousand Buddhas to celebrate this festivity.

The plans for the City of Ten Thousand Buddhas are ambitious. Aside from housing the Tathagata Monastery, the Great Compassion House for laymen who wish to study Buddhism and partake of its spirituality, and the Joyous Giving House for Buddhist nuns and laywomen, it is also the campus for the Dharma Realm Buddhist University.

This university, still in its fledgling stages, has approval to grant both undergraduate and graduate degrees in such areas as Buddhist studies, Asian languages, philosophy, and religion, and in the creative arts.

In addition, a home for the aged, a hospital emphasizing the utilization of both eastern and western healing techniques, and an alternative mental health facility are planned.

The progress on these programs is deliberately slow. Proper planning and sufficient resources for their implementation and maintenance are carefully considered. Nor should they impede the spiritual growth of the monastic community. "It is the inner life, the work of cultivation, that is important," Heng Kuan had told me at Gold Mountain Monastery. "When that is impeded, the light of the community goes out."

I walk to the Hall of Ten Thousand Buddhas, where the monks, nuns, and residents of the City of Ten Thousand Buddhas, along with numerous visitors, have gathered for a ceremony known as "the washing of the Buddha." Led by the Master Hsuan Hua, those assembled file out and walk around the grounds, chanting. A long line snakes around the buildings of the City of Ten Thousand Buddhas until it comes to a stream on the property. Monks bring forth some boxes containing turtles purchased a few days earlier in shops in San Francisco's Chinatown.

These creatures, which had been destined to end their days in soup tureens, are put on the banks of the stream in a liberation of life ceremony. In this ceremony, living creatures destined to be slaughtered are purchased and liberated. Fish and turtles, for example, are put in streams. Pigeons and doves are allowed to fly away.

"The ceremony is a practical application of compassion," Heng Lai tells me, "removing the obstacles of people's innately compassionate minds. The basic obstruction is the accumulation of resentment which can lead to the killing of other beings. When living beings are purchased and released, the act of killing is prevented, and hatred is lessened."

The turtles scamper into the stream. The venerable Master Hsuan Hua smiles. The monks, nuns, residents, and visitors join in the joy, which is more than the enjoyment of a symbolical act of saving some animals destined for destruction: there is a sense that the Buddha's compassion for life has come to the United States, and that the rigorously ascetic monks and nuns and other disciples of the Ch'an Master Hsuan Hua will effect a major transformation in this country.

Who can tell if a Buddhist master and teacher who speaks but little English, a Harvard honors student in literature, a seaman who had a profound religious experience on the deck of a boat, a "drop-out" from Chicago's West Side, a woman with a brilliant academic career in Oriental languages, a Chinese language student walking and bowing himself for several hundred miles, and others from diverse backgrounds can effect such a revolution?

The afternoon sun is sinking in the west as I leave the City of Ten Thousand Buddhas. The leaves on the streets of this former state hospital facility rustle in the breeze. What good is life, I wonder, if it does not consist of dreams and visions?

4

The Call to the Desert
The Spiritual Life Institute

THE drive north from Phoenix had been a pleasant excursion through the desert, but I was unprepared for the polychromatic austerity of Oak Creek Canyon, the varying shades of mysterious red rock mountains, and the verdant mesas surrounding the town of Sedona. The beauty of this Arizona desert was offset by the realization that it remained a vast, stern, uncharted, comfortless, burning bowl. Not even the creeping eczema of "ticky-tacky" housing developments could alleviate the beautiful harshness of this wilderness.

It is in the Oak Creek Canyon that a ranch, originally home-steaded in the early 1920s, has become the desert home for the Spiritual Life Institute, a monastic community that represents a return to that ideal of the first few centuries of Christianity that urged thousands to seek solitude in desert places and thus serve God through austerities and contemplation.

Nada (the Spanish word for *nothing*), as this modern experiment in the tradition of the desert fathers and the monks of Mt. Carmel is called, consists of seven acres and about a dozen rough and rustic buildings scattered about.

Aside from the old ranch house and the recently constructed

chapel, the buildings are small hermitages, each named after a favorite saint or hero of the Spiritual Life Institute—Thomas More, Don Quixote, Lao-tzu, Gandhi, Dag Hammarskjöld, and others. In these hermitages live the men and women who have chosen to lead a life memorialized by the Hebrew prophet Osee: "I will espouse you, lead you into the desert, and there I will speak to your heart" (Osee 2:14).

I am led to my hermitage—called Zhivago—by Tessa Bielecki, an attractive woman in her mid-thirties who has been a member of the community since the late 1960s. The small one-room structure contains a bed, a desk and chair, a sofa, a table, a small stove, cooking utensils, and a larder filled with food. A clothes closet and a bathroom complete the self-sustaining characteristics of this monastic cell.

I rapidly unpack, and Tessa and I sit in front of the secluded hermitage to discuss the Spiritual Life Institute. The vision of a Carmelite priest, Father William McNamara, the Institute was founded in 1960, when McNamara discussed his ideal for a contemporary community of hermits (a term that refers to monks seeking a life of solitude) with Pope John XXIII. The pope urged him to adhere to his idea at all costs. It was not until 1963, however, that McNamara was able to establish the beginnings of his experimental community in Sedona. Three years later, he purchased the nearby ranch property that the Institute now occupies as one of its two communities.

Reaching back to the earliest days of Christian monasticism—the third and fourth centuries—when thousands departed from the urban centers of the decaying Roman Empire and sought solitude in the deserts of Egypt, Syria, and Palestine, the Spiritual Life Institute has recreated the spirit and characteristics of primitive monasticism. It is a community of men and women, laypersons who make serious private vows within the community.

The Spiritual Life Institute claims affinity with the primitive Carmelite ideal. This group is described by Thomas Merton in *Disputed Questions* as follows:

> The first Carmelites had imitated something quite original and unique: a loose-knit community of hermits with an informal, occasional apostolate. . . .
> The Carmelites were originally hermits. And of course their life

was the traditional hermit life known to the east from the earliest centuries of the Church. They lived as the desert fathers had lived eight hundred years earlier. They began as an offshoot of the ancient, informal charismatic monachism of Syria and Palestine. But they were not monks in the western sense. . . . They were originally not cenobites. They had no liturgical office in common. They did not live in monasteries or cloisters. They were in fact simple laymen, living as solitaries in a loosely connected group, in caves and huts on the side of Mount Carmel.[1]

The Carmelites themselves did not preserve this original idea, becoming instead a religious order of mendicant friars; and the Spiritual Life Institute is itself more cenobitical (that is, clustered in an informal community) than eremitical. Nevertheless, the essential spirit of the eremitic ideal, based on primitive Christian monachism, seems preserved at Nada, and at the Institute's community in Nova Scotia, known as Nova Nada.

The element of a mixed community of men and women, although seemingly a concession to a contemporary egalitarian concept of the sexes, also is rooted in tradition: St. Jerome was accompanied by woman when he retreated to a monastic life; and double-minsters, as they were known (separate but adjoining monasteries for men and women), were not unusual during the first several centuries of Christianity.

Tessa describes the Spiritual Life Institute as "a constantly evolving way of life." And, indeed, this community is difficult to pigeonhole within a framework of familiar monastic groups and concepts. This use of a monastic habit at the Institute did not come about until 1972; and it is worn today only at liturgical functions. There are as yet no written rules of life or constitutions. Instead, the community lives "in the spirit of a family," as Tessa describes it, relying on the direction of the Holy Spirit through the charismatic leadership of its founders. "We are committed," she says, "to annihilation of the false ego, a kind of self-actualizing surrender." Traditional vows of poverty, chastity, and obedience are taken by members of the community and renewed each year. At least five years in the community are required before vows for life can be taken.

Celibacy is not a definitive requirement. The Spiritual Life In-

1. Thomas Merton, *Disputed Questions* (London: Hollis & Carter, 1961), pp. 218-219.

stitute is opposed to the idea that celibacy is a higher spiritual calling than marriage, and foresees married couples (but not children) as being part of the community in the future.

The sun is high overhead as Tessa and I walk through the few trees that dot Nada, along a stony trail, towards the chapel. The journey that led her to the Spiritual Life Institute, she says, began when she was a student at Trinity College in Washington, D.C., majoring in Russian. An excellent student with an active social life, Tessa attended a student retreat conducted by McNamara. "I recognized him as a towering human being, a man of great holiness and humility, and a remarkable spiritual leader," she tells me. "I wanted to discover what he obviously had: nothing less than the Living God. I knew intuitively and immediately that my vocation lay with the Spiritual Life Institute."

The chapel at the Spiritual Life Institute's community in Arizona's Oak Creek Canyon harmonizes with the austere landscape.

However, McNamara insisted that she finish her college education and work one year before joining the Spiritual Life Institute. She did so, and in 1967 joined the Institute in Arizona.

We arrive at the chapel—a stone structure in a contemporary architectural style that blends in admirably with the desert envirionment—where mass will be said shortly by a diocesan priest from Utah who has been staying at Nada for the past year. He is attempting to discover whether he has a vocation to the life of contemplative solitude. Tessa tells me in an almost embarrassed manner that mass is not celebrated every day. Traditionally, the core of the spiritual life for Catholics has centered around daily mass and communion. And yet, such a tradition is superseded by the tradition of the desert monks of the third century as exemplified by St. Antony, the most renowned of these early hermits, who neither went to church nor received the sacraments for years, but nevertheless continued in closest union with God. Also in the third century, at Nitria, some fifty miles southeast of Alexandria in the Nile Delta, eight priests sufficed for the spiritual administration of five thousand monks.

Tessa and I enter into the chapel by way of a striking, high-beamed, large room that serves as a library, and descend a narrow flight of steps into a plain, stone room half submerged beneath the ground. A portable altar and a tabernacle are its only adornments. One is reminded of the "kivas" of the Indians of the Southwest. A solitary person is sitting cross-legged in a corner of the room, eyes closed, dwarfed in this chapel with its tall ceiling.

Following Tessa's lead, I make profound bows in the direction of the tabernacle; and then she excuses herself to put on her habit. Within a few moments the chapel begins to fill with members of the community, as well as those who have come to Nada for spiritual retreats of varying lengths of time. There are no chairs in the chapel, and the dozen persons who have gathered sit cross-legged against a wall.

Mass is celebrated quite simply. The priest officiates, and Tessa and another member of the community read the epistle and gospel. Some of the group file out silently after the conclusion of mass; others stay in quiet contemplation.

I return to my hermitage to prepare lunch. Only a few meals during the week are eaten in common at the Spiritual Life Institute; all other meals are prepared in one's hermitage. I fiddle with the hot plate, heat some soup, pour some juice into a glass, and eat my simple fare at the table, looking out across Oak Creek Canyon and listening to the midday stillness.

Following the inspiration of the orignal Carmelite hermits, the Institute is characterized by simplicity and a minimal structure to enable members to offer God a pure and undivided heart. There are times when total solitude prevails for an entire week. At such times, there are no meals in common and no common prayer. A more typical week will see the community gather together for morning and evening prayer, mass, and a few common meals, with mornings devoted to solitude and afternoons to manual labor in the kitchen, office, or garden. To emphasize playing and praying as man's two highest acts because of their pure nonutility, whenever possible one full day a week is given over to recreation, and the members of the community play volleyball, go for a hike, or engage in some other recreational activity.

In the mid-afternoon I wander out of my hermitage to stroll through Nada. Near the ranch house, a water pump is being installed by Father Michael Winterer, the diocesan priest who has been residing at Nada for a year. Maureen Reilly, who is soon to be admitted as a member of the community, is weeding in a large garden area. In a nearby hermitage, a structure that formerly had been the root cellar for the ranch, Patricia McGowan is typing address labels for *Desert Call*, the quarterly magazine published by the Spiritual Life Institute.

I knock on the door of her hermitage and ask if I may speak with her. She bids me come in, and I enter the tiny, half-underground structure and sit on a wooden chair while Pat McGowan prepares me a cup of tea. A member of the Spiritual Life Institute since 1971, she was born in Chicago, was educated by nuns of the Dominican order, and entered a convent after high school. In 1970, she experienced a crisis in her vocation—a crisis she attributes to the rapid changes that took place in Catholicism following Vatican Council II—and shortly thereafter she went to Nada for a retreat of almost a month. She returned to the Spiritual Life Institute the following year, and stayed for four years before deciding to leave her order and become a member of the community of the Spiritual Life Institute.

"I felt that the Institute was the fullness of my religious vocation," she tells me. "It was a difficult decision to make. However, I felt that God was calling me to a life of contemplative solitude."

The call to a life of contemplative solitude is one that has become more common among members of Catholic religious orders and members of the diocesan clergy during the past few years. Sister Patricia Kelley, a member of the Sisters of Charity of the Incarnate Word, had a desire for a period of solitude. For nine years her superiors refused her permission. They finally relented and allowed her to spend a year at Nada.

"I don't have a call to stay here always," she says while hanging laundry on a clothesline, "but I did have a vocation for a year of solitude. After the year is over, I go back to my own community."

As I begin to wander back to my hermitage, Maureen Reilly is completing her weeding. Pigtailed and freckled, she tells me that she is from the San Francisco Bay Area and had attended two Bay Area colleges that I know well. Her introduction to the Spiritual Life Institute took place when she was in college and attended a retreat given by Father McNamara.

"After the retreat, I felt that I would like to come to Nada," she tells me, "and I decided that I needed a break. In January of 1975, I went to Nova Nada in Nova Scotia, and spent five months there. I returned there for a year from mid-1976 to mid-1977. And now I'm here at Sedona. I've just made my first vows, and I plan to spend the rest of my life as a member of the Institute."

A good student with an interest in writing, tennis, swimming, and jogging, Maureen indicates that she didn't feel any vocation to the religious life before she came to the Spiritual Life Institute. Nor did she feel that the life of contemplative solitude held any interest for her.

"But I guess that's what God had intended for me," she says, "because the Institute has become the way in which I could best live out my ideals."

The sun slips behind the mesas of Oak Creek Canyon, highlighting the many shades of red in the massive rocks. I enter my hermitage and wait for Tessa Bielecki, who is coming to discuss the Institute and its aims at greater length.

She enters dressed in her habit—a simple brown robe with a headdress that covers her black hair—for there is to be evening prayer and supper in common this evening.

I express my astonishment at the lifestyle within the Spiritual Life Institute—where, aside from assigned work tasks and occasional gatherings for mass, prayer, and meals, everyone seems to be left to his or her own devices.

"Don't forget," she reminds me, "that this was the earliest tradition of monasticism. We feel that the only way one learns how to pray is to listen to the Holy Spirit, by going out and praying. After all, Christ didn't exactly 'teach' us to pray but induced us to live, sure as He was that if we immerse ourselves in being, willing to be wounded as well as uplifted, we will indeed pray. The Institute is a group of hermits bound together by the charismatic leadership of its founder and leader, and Father William, although the demands of his apostolate mean that he isn't always in the community, is our spiritual director. Again, this is in the tradition of the desert monks and the primitive Carmelites, who would gather around a monk renowned for his extraordinary spirituality."

The unique qualities of the Spiritual Life Institute are very much the subject of our conversation. Can monastic community exist for long witout a more definitive rule of life? Don't those who are interested in the eremitical life at the Institute get "turned off" if there isn't more personal direction and contact? Can a spiritual community have any long-term existence without a canonical constitution? How does the fact that persons may come to Nada for nondirected retreats allow the community's members to live lives of solitude? Does the small number of those who have elected to become permanent members of the Institute indicate that this monastic experiment is too radical?

Tessa Bielecki answers my questions with both patience and a well-thought-out format — as if these questions have been posed before and discussed within the community. Darkness has enveloped Oak Creek Canyon as we conclude our discussion and walk towards the chapel for evening prayer. Our flashlights flicker in the blackness as we enter the grey stone structure. In the chapel, candles and dim lights cast a strange glow on the outlined figures wrapped in silence, waiting for evening prayer to begin. Pat McGowan leads the ancient psalms that comprise the bulk of this vocal prayer, and, after its conclusion, we all file out once more into the dark night.

The laughter and chatter in the ranch house, where the Spiritual Life Institute's community, retreatants, and guests have gathered for an evening meal in common, contrast with the quiet and solitude that I had hitherto witnessed. A well-cooked, ample, but frugal meal is served. The conversation is exuberant but not frivolous. Each person contributes to clearing the table after supper, washing and wiping the dishes. And then each one quietly departs for his or her hermitage.

Tessa offers to walk me to my hermitage. We stroll for a few minutes in silence, and then she says, "I know much of what we're doing here is difficult for you to comprehend: it's so different from what people have experienced in the Church. But our aim is to leaven and revolutionize the Church through what British theologian Rosemary Haughton calls 'creative subversion'—in the same way as the Church has always been enlivened throughout history by monasticism and mysticism. Aldous Huxley has said that the only effective way to change the world is through contemplation; and the Spiritual Life Institute aims at setting the stage for this contemplation, and allowing a profound transformation—in individuals' lives and in the world—to happen."

Tessa departs into the darkness after she has walked me to my door. I linger outside for a moment, looking at the whiteness of the countless stars above me. Truly, the desert is conducive to contemplation.

A few months after my visit to Nada in Arizona, I fly from Boston to Yarmouth, Nova Scotia, where I am to spend some time at Nova Nada, the Spiritual Life Institute's other community. Tessa Bielecki is there again—along with another permanent member of the community, David Denny—to meet me at the small airport, and to drive me to the former hunting and fishing lodge on the wooded banks of a lake that is the Spiritual Life Institute's second outpost of solitude.

The difference between this frozen, snow-covered wilderness and Oak Creek Canyon is startling. Our truck bounces along the rutted road, and in an hour and a half we arrive at Nova Nada. Most of the buildings are left from the property's previous status as a hunting and fishing lodge. A chapel is in the final stages of construction. Within a few months, the entire community of the Spiritual Life Institute will be centered at Nova Nada for an intense period of solitude and formation.

Dave Denny trudges with me across the snow-covered ground to my hermitage. In his late twenties, Denny was born and raised in Indiana. His family moved to Arizona while he was in high school; and his interest in religion grew while he attended the University of Arizona, majoring in Middle Eastern studies. Raised in the Methodist faith of his parents, Denny rejected Protestantism for what he feels is the missing element of mysticism. He plunged into the study of Eastern metaphysics and religions; but it was his roommate's gift of Thomas Merton's autobiography, *Seven Storey Mountain*,[2] that identified his monastic leanings. This reading experience, coupled with his spending a few days at Nada at a friend's urging, galvanized a religious crisis, at which time he began to ask himself ultimate questions about the purpose of his life. The result was his joining the Spiritual Life Institute in early 1975, his conversion to Catholicism later that year, and his decision to make a lifetime commitment to the Institute's eremitical community.

He leaves me to do my unpacking in the rustic hunting cabin—now named Charles de Foucauld—that serves as my hermitage. The familiar hot plate and food larder are part of the cabin's furnishings—which also include a bed, a desk that looks out over the vast frozen lake, and an old stuffed chair. But even the cabin bespeaks the difference between Nada and Nova Nada: life is tougher and more rigorous in this Nova Scotia wilderness. I notice that the sink, shower, and toilet have no running water; and that water has to be brought in from a nearby well. I notice that the various construction projects—of new hermitages and the chapel—must call forth from the Institute's hermits much more physical labor than in Arizona. Maintenance of life in these northern woods, particularly during the winter, seems to demand far more stamina. I am reminded of a passage from Henry David Thoreau:

> I went to the woods because I wished to live deliberately, to confront only the essential facts of life. . . . I wanted to live deep and suck out all the marrow of life, to live so sturdily and Spartan-like as to put to rout all that was not life, to cut a broad swath and shave close, to drive life into a corner and reduce it to its lowest terms. . . . For most men, it appears to me . . . have somewhat hastily concluded that it is the chief end of man here to "glorify God and enjoy Him forever."

There is a knock on the door. I open it, and see standing there a young man, bearded and smiling.

"Hi, I'm David Levin. It's great to meet you at long last."

He comes in, removing his heavy coat, his gloves, and the boots that he has worn to tramp through the snowdrifts. His handsome,

2. Thomas Merton, *Seven Storey Mountain*, (New York: Harcourt, Brace & World, 1948).

prophetlike face is made more intense by the gold-rimmed glasses he is wearing.

I brew some coffee on the wood stove that serves to heat my hermitage, and sit and talk with this recently ordained priest, who has been at the Spiritual Life Institute since 1968. Born in 1948, David Levin lived with his mother in New York and New Jersey until he was thirteen. Then he went to live with his father, a successful Hollywood movie director, in California and Europe.

Levin spent part of his high-school years at a private boarding school in Sedona, Arizona, where he met Father William McNamara. After a stint in college, Levin went to Los Angeles to work for Columbia Pictures.

"In 1968," Levin tells me, "I wanted to change my life. A friend of mine called me one day and invited me to accompany him on a weekend at the Spiritual Life Institute. I went along with him and underwent such a profound transformation in my life while I was there that I decided to stay."

Levin lived at Nada in Arizona from 1968 until 1972, when he went to Nova Scotia to help found Nova Nada.

"In 1973, I left the Institute for six months to examine my vocation in another environment. I returned, took my vows for a permanent commitment to the Institute in 1974, and began to study for the priesthood."

Levin's studies for the priesthood have been unconventional. He was baptized a Roman Catholic in 1969—the year after he had decided to become a member of the Spiritual Life Institute community—and decided in 1974 that he also had a call to the priesthood. Under the guidance of Father McNamara, he studied those subjects that are part of traditional seminary curricula, and then he went to live and study at St. Joseph's Abbey in Spencer, Massachusetts. At the conclusion of his theological studies at this Cistercian monastery, Levin was ordained a priest by the bishop of Yarmouth, Nova Scotia.

Up to now, Father Levin has been immersed in the construction tasks that have been necessary both in Arizona and Nova Scotia; but his ordination, he believes, will alter his role somewhat.

"But ordination does not change the fact that I am a hermit at the Spiritual Life Institute, that my vocation is to live a life of solitude and contemplation," he says.

He goes on to describe the importance of this life for contemporary society.

"The Spanish word *nada*, which means 'nothing,' was chosen for our communities because nothing, the abyss, the void, is the experience of the wilderness. Nothingness is also the one mystery in which all religious traditions—East and West—converge. St. John of the Cross and others sum up the spiritual life in terms of it: unless you are detached from everything that is not God, you cannot belong to God; unless you are emptied, you cannot be filled; unless you lose your life, you cannot find it.

"Nothingness may save or destroy those who face it, but those who ignore it are condemned to unreality. They cannot pretend to a real life, which, if it is full of real risks, is also full of real promises.

"A person has to pull out of the human anthill, the asphalt jungle, the daily chase; he has to become present to himself. He cannot give what he does not have. Self-possession is not the end, but it must happen along the way or one will never get to the end, at least not a distinctively worthy human end. He has to expose himself to the world of wisdom, the world of piety—not a flurry of pietistic talk, books, and practices, but to the communion of saints characterized by a wild, fierce, passionate devotion to the deepest human possibilities, the mysterious summons of God."

Levin's earnestness has made me oblivious to the furious boiling of the coffee pot. I pour two cups of steaming coffee. Outside, It has begun to snow again. I ask Levin whether such an individualistic approach to the spiritual life does not mean that a spiritual community is not necessary.

"The Spiritual Life Institute is eremitical," he responds. "We have chosen to live together alone. It is nearly impossible to be a hermit on your own, for practical as well as psychological reasons. We live together to provide the mutual supports needed to overcome the difficulties we would encounter without other hermits living nearby. We avoid the degree of organization needed for 'community,' yet maintain a simple structure which enables us to help one another be hermits without hindering one another.

"We protect one another's solitude both from deteriorating into loneliness and from being infringed upon by misguided or disordered togetherness. Paradoxically, we enjoy genuine community precisely because we are solitaries: togetherness without solitude is merely side-by-sideness. Genuine community is not a self-conscious looking at one another, but a self-oblivious looking beyond ourselves to the One who draws us together as He binds us to Himself."

A member of the Spiritual Life Institute's "Nova Nada" community in Nova Scotia meditates in the chapel.

Levin goes on to explain that the life of solitude is not a selfish rejection of the world. "The hermit is not a caveman or a spook, luxuriating in isolated splendor," he continues. "He does not flee from the world to be free of it, but enters into it to transfigure it; he does not scorn the good pleasures of the world, but integrates them with the spiritual. He aims not at rejection out of fear, but consecration born of love. It is not merely for his own benefit that he enters into solitude, but for the sake of the entire world: to pray for the world, to be witness to the world, to provide the world with a silent and solitary atmosphere of prayer."

We finish our coffee, and Levin departs. I watch him disappear into the snowstorm, walking towards his hermitage.

During my final days at Nova Nada, I live in virtual solitude, experiencing a life that is unusual in the twentieth-century world. I cook on my hot plate, drag pails of water into my hermitage, feed the wood-burning stove with logs from a pile in front of my dwelling, read—and contemplate. Occasionally, I take a walk on the frozen lake or through the monochromatic whiteness of the woods. On days of communal prayer, I am summoned early in the morning and early in the evening by a bell in front of the log cabin that now serves as a chapel, and I go to join the handful of hermits gathered there to recite the day's prayers. The sound of voices is unusual; but I welcome the recitation of the cadenced rhythm of the psalms.

Leaving Nova Nada, driving once more down the road to Yarmouth, I am reminded of the words of Thomas Merton that the solitary "is not called to leave society but to transcend it; not to withdraw from the fellowship with other men, but to renounce the appearance, the myth of union in diversion in order to attain to union on a higher and more spiritual level—the mystical level of the Body of Christ."[3]

As an understanding of early monasticism necessitates a comprehension of man's innate yearning for self-surrender coupled with the Christian's vision of spiritual combat, so does an understanding of the aims and ideals of the Spiritual Life Institute involve an understanding of the traditional Christian values of self-renunciation and the determination to follow and imitate Christ.

3. Merton, *Disputed Questions*, p. 182.

5

From Baba with Love

Om Namah Shivaya
Om Namah Shivaya
Om Namah Shivaya

THE chant is repeated over and over, hour after hour, in the large, darkened meditation room at the ashram in Oakland, California. About one hundred and fifty men and women, virtually all of them in their twenties and thirties, sway slightly as they chant, accompanied by a variety of exotic instruments: a harmonium, drums, tambouras, cymbals, and lartels.

One verse is chanted by the women, seated on one side of the room; the other verse by the men, seated on the other side. They sit in the cross-legged yoga position, facing a shrine consisting of a large, turquoise velvet-covered throne holding a color photograph of Swami Muktananda Paramahansa, decorated with flowers, illuminated with candles, and scented with burning incense. A pair of Muktananda's sandals, some glass elephants, and other objects associated with him rest at the foot of the spotlighted throne. Above the throne is a large photograph, framed by a string of small blue lights, of Muktananda's predecessor as the Guru of the Siddha Yoga lineage, Bhajawan Nityananda. And photographs of other Gurus in this lineage, similarly lighted, cover the walls of the thickly carpeted room. In the back of the room is a long table on which sit elegant silver trays, bowls, and candelabra. Fruit, flowers, and burning incense are arranged around the silver utensils.

It is a weekend of "Saptah"—an intense, ongoing period of chanting and meditation held at least once a month at the ashram. The one hundred men and women who live here, and devotees and followers of Muktananda who live elsewhere, have gathered to chant and meditate at variously scheduled hours.

In a decaying neighborhood in the large industrial city of Oakland, in what was once a ramshackle hotel-turned-flophouse, is the Oakland Siddha Yoga Dham, or ashram (meaning spiritual community), the largest of the Muktananda ashrams in the United States, and the headquarters for Muktananda's religious organization in the United States. It was here that Swami Muktananda, known as "Baba" to his followers, lived for a year in 1975 and 1976, during a two-year peregrination through North America and Europe before returning to India in October, 1976.

To enter the ashram, residents press a buzzer, going in only after identifying themselves over an intercom. Halfway up a long flight of stairs, you deposit your shoes and proceed in stocking feet.

In the maze of corridors on the second floor are a library and a series of former hotel rooms—now the residences of those who have chosen to live in the ashram. Another long flight of stairs leads to the third floor, on which are the offices of the ashram and of the national S.Y.D.A. (Siddha Yoga Dham Ashram) Foundation, conference rooms, and additional rooms for the community's inhabitants. Dark wooden floors, waist-high wooden paneling, and white-painted walls create an atmosphere of somber peace.

The tranquility pervading the ashram is broken only by the sound of chanting coming from hidden loudspeakers. The occasional person you meet in the corridors greets you simply with a smile and a nod. Conversation is kept to a minimum.

The first floor contains two meditation halls, a large kitchen, an adjoining dining hall, storerooms, and a bookstore. A walk down another long corridor leads one to a courtyard and an annex of the building. It was in this annex, with its decorated facade, that Muktananda lived in 1975-76; and his rooms are maintained as they were while he was in residence.

The departure of Muktananda for his ashram at Ganeshpuri in India has meant a decline in the thousands of his followers and visitors, including Governor Edmund G. Brown, Jr., singer John Denver, astronaut Edgar Mitchell, *est* guru Werner Erhard, and anthropologist Carlos Castaneda, who flocked to the Oakland ashram. Nevertheless, Muktananda's presence pervades the ashram. Photographs of him and of his predecessors as Siddha Yoga Gurus abound throughout the rooms of the building. The conversation of residents is sprinkled with references to Muktananda as a living presence in their lives.

Although he had traveled to Europe and the United States in 1970, it was Muktananda's two-year journey from 1974 to 1976 that precipitated the large following that continues today. Major articles about him appeared in *Time, Newsweek*, and other publications. Scores of devotees followed him in the United States, in Europe—and even to India after his return.

There are today an estimated 15,000 followers of Muktananda in the United States. Of these, a few hundred have elected to live in one of the five ashrams in the United States or in one of the meditation centers that have small residential communities. Most of the 230 meditation centers are not residential, however, and only center leaders live there.

The growth of Siddha Yoga as a spiritual force in the United States is one of the phenomena of the contemporary religious reawakening. The man who has sparked this religious enthusiasm was born in the southern part of India in 1908, left his home at the age of fifteen in quest of spiritual knowledge, and wandered throughout India mastering many of the yogic arts, meeting many of the country's spiritual leaders, and studying the Hindu scriptures. In 1947, he encountered Nityananda, the spiritual leader of Siddha Yoga, and shortly thereafter received initiation from him. For the next nine years, as Muktananda reveals in his autobiography, *The Play of Consciousness*,[1] his discipleship led to his final spiritual unfolding and a profound transformation.

These experiences culminated in 1956 with the attainment of self-realization, liberation, or Siddhahood. Nityananda raised Muktananda to his own level of Guru. In 1961, when Nityananda

1. Muktananda, *The Play of Consciousness*, (Camp Meeker, Calif.: SYDA Foundation, 1974).

died, Muktananda stood as his successor—the Guru of Siddha Yoga.

Yoga, in Hindu religious terminology, means union with that from which we have become alienated: the Supreme Being, God, the inner Self. It also means a method of achieving that union.

There are different yogas, or paths, for seekers of different temperaments. Jnana Yoga, for example, is the path of knowledge; Bhakti Yoga is the path of selfless service; Hatha Yoga, the path of physical discipline.

Siddha Yoga, according to Hindu religious belief, is the path that encompasses all other yogas. It is the yoga that is received from a Siddha, a perfected being, one who has realized his union with God. By virtue of this realization, a Siddha is a direct channel for the dispensation of divine grace. The seeker who receives that grace experiences purification in all levels of his being. In due course, the blocks that were keeping him from experiencing his own divinity are removed, and he recognizes himself as God.

The technical term used to describe this inner process is *kundalini awakening*. Kundalini is a conscious, intelligent energy—or "shakti"—that creates everything in the entire universe. It is the essence of every living thing.

The kundalini energy in man lies dormant at the base of his spine. Awakening this energy is the goal of all spiritual practices, all yogas, since, until this force is activated, man is unaware of his own true nature. He looks for happiness outside himself and he finds only frustration. Once the kundalini is awakened, man discovers the happiness inside. He becomes aware that he is "shakti," that he is God, and that everything else in the universe is God, too. His responses to his physical environment and his fellow men become positive, and he discovers extraordinary contentment within himself.

Methods for awakening the kundalini differ among the various yogas. With Siddha Yoga, kundalini awakening comes through the grace of the Siddha Guru. A miracle takes place, according to Siddha Yoga belief, when the seeker surrenders himself to the Guru. Then the kundalini "shakti" takes charge of the aspirant, removes his deficiencies and imperfections, and enlarges him limitlessly.

Obviously, then, the role of the Guru for followers of Siddha

Yoga is essential. And this explains the intense relationship between Muktananda and his devotees. A Guru is different from an ordinary teacher or instructor because his concern is not to impart mere intellectual knowledge, spiritual techniques, or physical skills to his disciples. A Guru is one who has the power to transmit his own experience of Self-realization to a disciple. The process by which he does this is called "shaktipat." The Guru transmits his own "shakti," or energy, into his disciples, thereby awakening the disciples' dormant kundalini energy. He can bring about this energy transmission by a touch, a word, a look, or even just a thought.

Once the kundalini is awakened, a true Guru helps and protects the disciple until he achieves perfection. Perfection is reached when one is anchored in God-consciousness, perceiving Him everywhere, in everything and in every creature.

Eschewing a split between worldliness and spirituality, and dispensing with the austere practices of many of the Indian spiritual paths, Siddha Yoga has displayed great appeal for young Americans; and Muktananda's genius has been to adapt Siddha Yoga to contemporary Western culture.

The blowing of a conch shell awakens the community at the Oakland ashram at 4:30 A.M. Residents wash and dress and appear in the meditation hall half an hour later for an hour of meditation. "Meditation is very necessary for man," writes Muktananda, ". . . the being who has drunk this nectar of meditation is always in ecstasy."

Breakfast follows at 6 A.M. Members of the ashram pick up trays and silverware and file past two windows where they are given the first of three ample vegetarian meals for the day. A sign proclaims that one may take all he or she wishes to eat but that one must eat all one takes. No food is wasted at the ashram.

Those working in the kitchen as part of their community duties have been preparing breakfast while other devotees have been at meditation. They serve the meal to the hundred members of the ashram and the handful of guests who come through the line, clear-eyed and smiling for such an early hour, chanting "Sri Ram, Jay Ram, Jay Jay, Ram Om" as they obtain their food.

Breakfast is eaten in silence. Devotees then return their trays,

The shrines to the gurus of the Siddha Yoga lineage permeate even the efficient kitchen of the Muktananda ashram.

plates, and silverware to the kitchen, where a designated crew will wash them, and once more congregate in the meditation hall to chant the "Guru Gita," the longest and most indispensable text chanted during the day. "The 'Guru Gita' is a supreme song of Shiva, of salvation," writes Muktananda. "It is a veritable ocean of bliss in this world. It encompasses the science of the Absolute, the yoga of the Self. It gives vitality to life. It is a harmonious composition; its 181 stanzas in varied verse patterns beautifuly describe the importance of devotion to the Guru, his role, his nature, and his distinguishing characteristics. If one who is devoted to the Guru sings this song, he easily attains all powers, realizations and knowledge, fulfilling the aim of yoga."

Those assembled sit cross-legged, books held in the right hand for those few who have not memorized the text. Nobody looks around or moves—except for swaying as the chant goes on.

I am surprised by both the memory of the members of the ashram and their ability to pronounce easily the difficult Sanskrit words:

Om asya srigurugita stotra mantrasya
    bhagavan sadasiva rsih

Nanavidhani chandamsi
    sriguruparamatma devata

Ham bijam sah saktih krom kilakam
    sriguru prasada siddhyarthe jape viniyogah

Hamsabhyam parivrtta patra kamalair
    divyair jagat karanair,
Visvot kirnamaneka dehanilayaih
    svacchandam atmecchaya;

Tadyotam padasambhavam tu caranam
    dipankura grahinam,
Pratyaksaksara vigraham gurupadam
    dhyayed vibhum sasvatam.

Thus the chant begins, and continues for 181 more verses.

By 9 A.M, the "Guru Gita" is finished, and it is time for "Guru-seva"—the work period. It is now that the difference between traditional Christian spiritual communities and the Eastern religious experience in the United States becomes apparent: almost all of the residents of the ashram work at jobs. They trot out to these jobs following the chanting of the "Guru Gita" and return to the ashram at the end of the day. This bifurcation of life is due to Muktananda's insistence that there should not be a separation between the "worldly" and the "spiritual," and also to the economic necessities of being able to support oneself in a spiritual community. For a handful of residents, however, their jobs consist of full-time work tasks at the ashram. Managers, accountants, and other positions that involve the management of the ashram and the operation of the S.Y.D.A. Foundation keep this small group at the ashram during the day.

I take the opportunity to talk with Sudama—the Hindu spiritual name received from Muktananda by Peter Sitkin. Sudama, born in 1940, met Muktananda in 1975, during a period when he had given up the practice of law and was on a spiritual search. A friend had taken him to the ashram, and he had taken an "Intensive"—a two-day introduction to Siddha Yoga, consisting of chanting, meditation, and talks. Sudama describes the experience as "powerful," producing "internally emanating bliss."

As Sudama talks, he twists the prayer beads he is holding in his hands. Jewish, Brooklyn-born, Cornell- and Columbia Law School-educated, Sudama is also a former partner of Sidney Wolinsky and Anthony Kline in forming the Public Advocates in San Francisco. As with Kline, a highly placed official in the administration of Governor Edmund G. Brown, Jr., and others of his associates, Sudama's intensity reflects well-honed legal skills and a passionate concern for social justice.

"I had great success as an attorney," he says, "owned two houses, had all the material benefits I ever dreamed about, but still felt unfulfilled."

This malaise—and his separation from his first wife in 1971—caused Sudama to change his life in 1971. He began a spiritual odyssey, principally becoming involved in yogic practices in San Francisco; and he later moved to Mendocino.

Meeting Muktananda transformed Sudama's life. He moved into the Oakland ashram, where he was to live until he remarried. He now lives across the street from the ashram, teaches part-time at Boalt Hall, the University of California at Berkeley's law school, maintains a small private practice, and is the lawyer for Muktananda's operation in the United States as well.

"Work is now part of my spiritual practice," Sudama relates. "I get caught up in my work, and then I come back through chanting, meditation, and the day's discipline."

Although he no longer lives at the ashram, Sudama considers it central to his spiritual life. "Our house is Baba's home," he states, "but the ashram helps me to keep contact with the centering in my life that Baba started."

One gets the impression that Sudama lives in his own residence out of convenience—his children visit him with some frequency—but that the ashram remains central to his life. His legal duties for Muktananda involve his presence there, and his schedule includes participation in the chanting and meditation sessions held at the ashram. He and his wife eat frequent meals at the ashram, and, as with many of Muktananda's followers who do not reside there, they live their lives according to the schedule kept at the ashram.

It is now noon, and the time has come for the noon chant. I walk down the two long flights of stairs to the smaller of the two meditation halls. There are fewer persons there than there were for the "Guru Gita," but about forty are soon chanting the basic mantra, "OM Namah Sivaya," "OM I bow to my Self."

At 12:30, I join those who had been chanting for lunch. Once more the devotees chant as they pass through the line and are served the food. The meal is taken in silence; but I sit with Agastya, the manager of the ashram, and discuss with him the day-to-day operations of the spiritual community.

Tall and reserved, Agastya, whose name was Dana Wilkinson, was born in 1950. A part-owner of a vegetarian restaurant in Ann Arbor, Michigan, after he had spent two years at Wayne State University in Detroit, Agastya had led an austere life of yoga and other spiritual practices before he met Muktananda during the latter's tour of the United States. Agastya's desire to follow Muktananda was immediate; and he traveled with him to New York, where he worked in the kitchen in the New York ashram. In March, 1976, Muktananda appointed Agastya manager of the Oakland ashram and secretary of the S.Y.D.A. Foundation.

"A true disciple sees his Guru everywhere," Agastya tells me. And the literal truth of this is to be seen in the Oakland ashram, in which there are hundreds of photographs and paintings of Muktananda—in the meditation halls, in the corridors, in the kitchen, in the dining hall, and in the rooms of the residents. "The Guru puts you in touch with your Self," he says earnestly. Once again, the role of the Guru as the essential catalyst for the discovery of divinity in oneself is touched on by one of Muktananda's followers.

Agastya's role is the physical operation of the ashram. The day-to-day existence of the hundred residents in this spiritual community is his bailiwick—food, lodging, the maintenance of discipline, the myriad details of maintaining the large physical plant. One cannot help being impressed by his competence if one spends any time in the ashram. The well-scrubbed neatness of the building, the regularity of the daily schedule, and the well-ordered, yet joyous, lives of the residents are a tribute to his skills.

The residents of the ashram are now "free" until 3 P.M. This period after lunch is used by some to rest, by others to take care of personal matters or to read, and for a handful to gather in Amrit, a small coffeehouse on the premises, to socialize.

I wander into Amrit, order a cup of tea, and chat with Dennis Guest, a tall, handsome, dark-haired dentist, who lives with his wife and daughter in the ashram.

Dennis has not taken a "new" name: "Because of my practice," he says, smiling shyly. His spiritual search began in the late 1960s. "I got into all sorts of things," he relates. "I read a great deal of mystical poetry, was into zen, meditation—and drugs. Then I read one of Baba's books, and realized three things: one, that everything I was doing was self-effort; two, that Baba was a very high saint; and three, that Baba could bestow profound spiritual experience. I decided to follow him."

One of the 75 percent of the residents of the ashram who has a job outside of the community, Dennis conducts his dental practice to fit the schedule of the ashram. "My family and I live here because it's a more conducive way for us to follow Baba's teachings," he states. "And it works out very well for us. The ability to devote our energies to the daily spiritual practices of Siddha Yoga is made possible by the communal division of labor here: the tasks of preparing and cooking food, of maintaining one's dwelling, and of all those domestic chores that have to be done in every household are here shared by the hundred people who live here. And they are done for the comunity as a whole."

As with many of the members of the Oakland ashram, Dennis

does not come from a religious background. "My father was a Baptist and my mother was Catholic," he says. "I guess you could say that I come from a 'low-key' religious family."

Did this lack of an intensive religious upbringing have anything to do with his spiritual search and with his commitment to Muktananda? "I guess I did feel starved for something which gave my life meaning beyond just going to school, making money, and living the usual day-to-day life I saw most people leading," he responds. "That's probably what got me interested in spirituality to begin with; and, when I encountered Baba, I felt I had found the answer to what meaning life had."

We are joined at our table by a blue-eyed, soft-spoken woman in her early thirties. She brushes back her light brown hair and smiles. "Am I disturbing you?" she asks. Her tranquil smile conveys joy and peace; and I assure her that she is welcome to sit and talk.

Vanita, born Roberta Citron, in response to my asking her about her life, tells me that she has a master's degree in special education and that she has both taught and worked in federal social programs. "I came to the conclusion that social programs, like the poverty programs, were band-aids."

Her decision to follow Muktananda was not preceded by any other spiritual quests. Divorced after a marriage of six years, Vanita met Muktananda in Oakland while he was living there, and she felt that her life had been transformed. She lived for a while at the ashram in Ganeshpuri, India, and then returned to the United States to live in the Oakland ashram. She supports herself now by working at a bagel stand in nearby Berkeley.

"I feel so lucky that this has happened to me. I'm totally satisfied. I love myself," she tells me as the three of us rise from the table.

It is almost 3 P.M.—and time once more for "Guruseva," working for the Guru. Those residents who are not employed elsewhere return to the jobs assigned them in the ashram. While a crew goes to the kitchen to begin preparing supper, others sweep the long corridors of the building and scrub the toilets and bathrooms. Those who work in the administrative and business offices return to their tasks, and a trio of ashramites turns to the painting of a first-floor storeroom.

I am struck by the absorption in their tasks that marks those performing them. A sense of alacrity and joy is invested in the work. It is almost as if a subtle shift in one's perceptions and intentions can transform even everyday, menial chores into important offerings.

As Dennis and Vanita depart to their assigned work, I walk up once more to the third floor for a meeting with the Swami Shantananda in one of the conference rooms.

Shantananda enters and greets me. He is dressed in the traditional orange robe of the Indian swami, over which he wears a pullover shirt and an open sweater. On his forehead is a red dot—the "tilak," a form of honoring the Guru as the flame of "shakti," he tells me—and three white, horizontal stripes, garnered from sacred ashes and representing the three basic qualities of nature. His head is shaved.

The bespectacled swami declines to discuss his life before his recent undergoing of "sannyasha" (the ritual by which Muktananda creates a swami, who is a special teacher and spiritual leader in the Hindu religious tradition) as one of the first five American swamis created by Muktananda—except to tell me that he is Puerto Rican. (The diverse composition of the followers of Muktananda in the United States is evident in the backgrounds of the five swamis: one Italian-American, two of Jewish origin, one black, and one Puerto Rican.) "That person is dead," he says, explaining his unwillingness to talk about his background.

Swami Shantananda is Muktananda's representative in both the Oakland ashram and the religious leader of Muktananda's followers in the western United States. His role involves traveling to Muktananda's meditation centers throughout the western states, to colleges and universities, and to spiritual centers, giving talks about Muktananda and Siddha Yoga. He is also involved in the Intensives given both at the Oakland ashram and in other places in the western United States, bestowing "shaktipat" (the transmission of spiritual power from Guru to disciple) in Muktananda's name on those who attend.

We discuss the role of the ashram in the broad context of Siddha Yoga. "The principal difference between an ashram in India and one in the United States," he says, "is that most of those who live in an ashram in the United States work at outside jobs. The effect of this is to spiritualize all that one does. The ashram serves as a vehicle for conveyance of 'the Guru's grace,' the awakening of the 'kundalini shakti.' And living in an ashram alleviates one's involvement in performing everyday tasks to be more free to perform the spiritual practices. But, as you know, Baba doesn't believe that the spiritual world is divorced from the world, and therefore no distinction is made between the person in the ashram and the person 'in the world.' "

The ceremony of "arati," showing honor to Baba Muktananda, begins late afternoon chanting at the Muktananda ashram.

I inquire about the rules for living in the ashram, how it is that that most difficult of living experiences — communal living — seems to function so smoothly.

"Introspection and awareness are the only rules," Shantananda replies. "People live at the ashram because they wish to pursue the

spiritual path of Siddha Yoga. If they don't wish to chant, to meditate, to live in harmony within the community, why stay? We have
certain rules that govern for the overall good of the ashram: for
example, there is a rule of silence, but it is a flexible rule; there is a
rule that permission has to be obtained for anyone who wishes to
stay out beyond 10 P.M.; and there is a requirement that all
residents partake in the work of the ashram. The success of the
community that you have observed is due to the spiritual transformation of those who live here."

We go on to discuss the unique role of the Guru in Siddha Yoga,
and Shantananda becomes intense and animated as he tells me:
"The Guru is one who perceives the divine and who leads the
aspirant to the discovery of his own divinity. Each one of us has
experienced a type of 'Guru' in our parents and teachers.

"Jesus was a Guru. And when the apostles had received his
Guru's grace on Pentecost, it was only after that that they went
forth to teach. But Christianity in the Western process has become
too juridical, has become cut off from the mystical.

"For us, surrender to the Guru is the link between all-pervasive
grace and ourselves."

Surrender is a word that is mentioned frequently by Muktananda's followers and in the literature of Siddha Yoga.

"To move from the role of seeker to the role of Siddha student,"
Shantananda elaborates, "you merely surrender. But surrender
does not imply giving up or losing your freedom. A Siddha is not
interested in creating disciples; he creates Siddhas. When the Guru
asks us to surrender, he is demanding that we give him our ego,
our doubts, our negativities, and our smallness. Baba once com-
pared the Guru to the 'merciful garbage truck,' which comes right
to our front door, picks up everything we don't want, and disposes
of it outside the city limits, never to be seen again.

"Nor is surrender a form of passivity. Right effort for the Siddha
student consists of regular meditation, chanting, mantra repetition,
and the subtle application of the Guru's highest teaching to ourselves and the world around us."

The late afternoon shadows are lengthening outside the ashram
as Swami Shantananda and I conclude our conversation and walk
downstairs to one of the meditation halls. It is 5 P.M. — and once
more time for one of the spiritual exercises at the ashram.

Suddenly, the main lights in the meditation hall come on. Everybody stands up. A mighty blast of horns, a crashing of cymbals, and a drumroll awaken one to the auspiciousness of the moment. A young man comes down the center of the hall bearing a silver tray on which lighted candles and bowls of burning incense are placed, and, before the color photograph of Muktananda on his throne, he executes an intricate maneuver of holding aloft, lowering, and moving the tray from side to side. When he has completed this ceremony, he turns and walks to the back of the hall, where he deposits the tray. This is the ritual known as "arati," performed each evening and used to mark the auspiciousness of an occasion and to honor the Guru.

"Arati" is followed at 5:30 P.M. by an "open" chant (one that may be attended by visitors), and then, at 6 P.M., by the communal chant for residents of the ashram and those followers of Muktananda who live elsewhere.

At 6:45 P.M., dinner is served. This is the only meal of the day at which conversation is allowed. The line moves rapidly as those who have labored in the ashram all day are joined by those who have returned from their outside jobs. The dining hall rings with the joyful chatter of the eight children who live in the ashram, and with the restrained laughter and ebullient conversation of the adults.

I sit at one of the plain cafeteria tables across from Yashoda (Elizabeth Woods), an attractive, dark-haired woman in her late thirties, and her daughter Krishni. A transplanted New Yorker, Yashoda tells me that she had worked in advertising in New York City, had been married and divorced, and had met Muktananda in 1970.

"My life changed dramatically," she says. Her pretty, oval face glows as she recalls her meeting with the man who was to become her Guru. "Immediately, my goals changed from materialistic to spiritual. I had been pulled towards yoga before I met Baba, but hadn't had any spiritual inclinations that I was aware of."

In 1971, Yashoda moved with her daughter to Piedmont, California, where a community of Muktananda's followers was being established. She intensified her spiritual search in these communal surroundings and became more convinced that Muktananda was to be her Guru. In 1975, she moved into the just-completed ashram in Oakland.

Yashoda, who is an accountant in the ashram's business office, freely discusses her life in the ashram. "I have to be totally responsible," she says. "It's as if there are mirrors around, constantly reflecting what I'm doing, who I am. Living here is the central experience of my life—which is not to say it's not without difficulties. Whenever you live with a hundred persons, there are always going to be some abrasions.

"Another problem for me is combining the discipline at the ashram with joyful motherhood. But that works out well most of the time. Although she's only eight years old, Krishni shares the household duties and is assigned chores for the ashram; and she also chants."

"I'm Krishna's child," adds Krishni, looking at me with wide, smiling eyes.

"The purpose of a spiritual community is that it helps you love God," Yashoda continues. "And that is why I've elected to live in the ashram for the rest of my life. The specialization of my life here gives me the ability to chant and to love God. Krishni gets input from the other members of the ashram, and I'm also free to do things with her, taking her to the park, visiting her grandmother, and some of the other things that children like to do."

We finish eating our fruit—dessert following the exellent vegetarian supper—and I find myself wondering about this attractive, vital woman's social life. The celibacy required of the unmarried followers of Muktnanda—particularly those who reside in an ashram—seems at variance with contemporary culture in the United States; and I ask her about this.

"When you love God," she explains, "some things are given up, not because they're necessarily bad, but because they're incompatible with the all-consuming love that you've found. From a practical viewpoint, when you get up at 4 A.M., you can't stay up very late to go off on dates. And, frankly, I don't think I could get involved with anyone who isn't a follower of Baba.

"My becoming a follower of Baba has meant a redirection of my energy—it's been totally and dramatically a rebirth."

The three of us leave the table. Within a few moments it will be time for an optional chant, beginning at 7:30 P.M. Some of the ashramites will take the opportunity to accomplish personal chores, others will meet once again in one of the meditation halls to chant.

The evening program begins at 8 P.M., and all of the residents of the ashram file into the smaller of the two meditation halls for a program that varies from night to night. There may be a talk given by Swami Shantananda or some visitor of importance, a slide show or movie featuring Muktananda, or a period of meditation.

At 9 P.M., the program ends, and the residents of the ashram relax or once more attend to some personal matters until 9:30 P.M., when they reconvene in the meditation hall for the final spiritual exercise of the day—a half-hour chant, "Hare Rama." At its conclusion, all depart for their rooms. The conch shell sounds in the darkened ashram at 10 P.M. It is "lights out" for the residents of the ashram, who will awaken to another day in six and a half hours to the same trumpeting.

A Siddha Yoga ashram in the United States differs as a monastic community from a traditional Christian monastery or from other Christian spiritual communities, not in the intensity of commitment of those who elect to reside in one or in the discipline required of residents, but in the lack of formal requirements.

There are no official clothing regulations: only the swamis wear traditional Hindu garb; others dress in the contemporary style of casual clothing. Commitment to become a follower of Muktananda and to live in an ashram is accomplished quite simply: there are no vows, no novitiate training, no graduated steps leading to formal acceptance, no difficulties presented if one wishes to leave the community. The great number of those who commit themselves to live in a Siddha Yoga ashram work at outside jobs in order to support themselves.

There are other variations of spiritual community lifestyles among the followers of Muktananda. Leaving a successful career as an advertising executive in New York City, Michael Butler became a group leader at the Esalen Institute in Big Sur, California, where he met Muktananda and decided to follow the Siddha Yoga path. He lived in the Oakland and New York ashrams and at the Ganeshpuri ashram in India before taking an apartment in the San Francisco Bay Area, where he continues his work as a group leader. About two or three times a week, Butler will spend time at the Oakland ashram, partaking in the spiritual exercises and routine there.

"Despite my having left the ashram, I continue to live like a monk," he says. "I lead my groups for a living, and spend the rest of my life quite simply: meditating, studying, and going to the ashram. My social life is also quite simple: basically getting together occasionally with friends."

Yet another lifestyle is encountered at the Siddha Yoga Dham of San Francisco, one of more than two hundred Siddha Yoga meditation centers located throughout the United States. Most of these are meeting places for nearby followers of Muktananda to gather for chanting, talks, and meditation; and most are devotees' homes. Some, like that in San Francisco, are more formally constituted.

Begun in mid-1977 by three followers of Muktananda who had met at the Ganeshpuri ashram, this meditation center is what might be called a "mini-ashram." Four to six persons, including the three founders, live more or less collectively in the two flats of a building in San Francisco's Mission district. They follow a modified schedule based on that of an ashram and hold the flat open at specified times for devotees.

It was a foggy Sunday evening when I met Yogi Ram, Yamuna, and Rukmani, all in their late twenties, who had started the Siddha Yoga Dham of San Francisco. Sunday and Wednesday evenings are open to those followers of Muktananda who wish to attend programs. The average attendance is about twenty persons; although occasionally up to one hundred devotees and visitors squeeze into the flat for a program of chanting, meditation, and a talk.

I am greeted by Yogi Ram, take off my shoes in the entryway, and walk up a flight of stairs to the tidy flat. The living room has been converted into a meditation hall. A shrine of honor to Muktananda is located at one end of the room. Photographs of Muktananda and his predecessors are displayed on the walls. The dining room contains a selection of books and tapes for sale.

From a Jewish background in New York, Yogi Ram (Arnold Drogen) attended Union College, traveled in Africa on a fellowship, and attended graduate school in dramatic arts at the University of California at Berkeley, where he also taught. In 1974, while at Berkeley, he met Muktananda and subsequently engaged in a five-day meditation retreat. Two years later, he went to India and lived at Ganeshpuri for four months. It was there that he met

Yamuna and Rukmani and, with Muktananda's blessing, decided to return to the United States and begin the meditation center in San Francisco.

"I was not a spiritual seeker before I met Baba," says Yogi Ram, "but he made me see that there was more to my existence than what I had realized."

The lifestyle led by this handsome, engaging devotee is subordinated to his religious commitments. Yogi Ram and those who live in the meditation center rise early each morning, meditate from 6 to 7 A.M., and chant from 7 to 8 A.M. The founding trio of devotees works in spurts at a variety of jobs for their sustenance and to maintain the meditation center. Yamuna is a student at the California Institute of Asian Studies and a part-time counselor. Rukmani, who has degrees in English education and in theatre, has worked as a waitress and now sells in a boutique. Yogi Ram takes an occasional sales job.

Born in Florida, raised in New Jersey, from a "moderately religious" Jewish family, Yamuna (Abbey Rosen) received a degree in education from the American University in Washington, D.C., before going to graduate school in psychology at Boston University. She began working in a program for cooperative living, and started to meditate in 1971 after an introduction to Transcendental Meditation.

In 1974, Yamuna migrated to San Diego, where she worked as a counselor for the Y.M.C.A. and became involved in Arica, one of the myriad of human potential groups that exploded in popularity in the 1970s. It was while living at the Arica commune in San Diego that she met Muktananda.

"I got involved very slowly," says the pretty, dark-haired, ebullient devotee. "Muktananda told me that I should live alone, which I did. It was the first time in my life that I had done so. And then, in 1976, I decided to go to Ganeshpuri, where I stayed for eight months. It was there that I decided to follow Baba with all my being."

About forty devotees and visitors had by this time gathered in the flat. Yogi Ram gave a short introductory talk, and then the chanting began. The diverse group of mostly young persons in their twenties and thirties chanted to the accompaniment of drums, cymbals, tambouras, and a harmonium. A talk by a young woman who recently had returned from a stay at Ganeshpuri followed. When she concluded telling her experiences in India, Yogi Ram announced that there would be a period of socializing before the final chant. Carrot cake and tea were served to the group.

I took the opportunity to talk with Rukmani (Rebecca Taubert), tall, extremely attractive, brown-haired, and blue-eyed. From a large family in Indiana, Rukmani grew up in a religious Lutheran background. "I was very religious when I was a child," she informs me in her soft voice, "but I gave up religion when I was fifteen."

She attended the University of Illinois in Chicago, and in her sophomore year married an architect. She received her degree, taught, was involved in community theatre, and was divorced after four years of marriage. For six months she lived in Mexico with a man she had met after her divorce.

"When I returned to Chicago," she relates, "I broke up with this man. I was working the I Ching one day, and it said I would meet a great teacher. Almost immediately I was invited to hear Baba give a talk. I went, and it was a psychedelic experience. Never had I experienced something so powerful—something I was so certain about.

"I left shortly thereafter, and went to Oakland, where I helped get the ashram started. When Baba left for India, I went also and stayed there for four months."

The final chant is about to begin. Plates and cups are put down, and everyone gathers again in the living room. Rukmani performs the ritual of "arati"—the candles burning on the silver tray outlining her tall form in the darkened room. At about 10:30 P.M. the chant concludes, and the followers of Muktananda file out into the foggy evening.

Yogi Ram, Yamuna, and Rukmani clean the flat before going to bed. Like all those who commit themselves to follow Muktananda in a spiritual community, they must arise early the following morning.

6

The Gift of Community
Weston Priory

I look at the license plates on the automobiles in the parking lot as I walk from the guest house to the former hay barn, where on Saturdays and Sundays the monks of Weston Priory celebrate the Eucharist. The plates express a litany of New England and Middle Atlantic states and Canadian provinces. They have come from Maine and New Jersey and Pennsylvania; there are taciturn Vermonters and voluble New Yorkers. Eva Healy, in her mid-nineties, is there; so is Samantha Shane, a gurgling infant of four months. There are scores of children, students from Dartmouth, Brown, Amherst, and Boston College, retired couples, and young marrieds. A few people live nearby in the area of Weston, Vermont. Most have driven several hours.

About a thousand persons are gathered in the hay barn or under a roof adjacent to it when the seventeen monks of the Priory walk in and take their places at a semicircle of folding chairs in the middle of the barn. One of the monks says a few words of welcome.

Brother Augustine and Brother Gregory hold guitars. They begin to play, and the other brothers sing. When the song is finished, a brief litany and prayer are offered, after which another monk reads a selection from the Old Testament. The monks begin to sing again, and the congregation joins them. The monk who offered the prayer now reads a selection from the Gospel of St. Matthew.

There are a few moments of silence at the conclusion of this reading, and then one of the monks makes a few comments on the passage. Another period of silence. Then another monk delivers a very brief, spontaneous homily, tying together the two selections from Scripture. A woman sitting in the hay barn comments on the passage from St. Matthew.

The scene is reminiscent of a meeting of the Society of Friends. When no more comments are forthcoming, the monks sing another song—after which they walk from their chairs to a table, covered with a colorful tablecloth, on which are set four large pottery cups and a basket containing several loaves of bread.

The monks, each wearing a cowl, a robe with wide sleeves, and a hood (left back), flank Brother John, the prior of Weston Priory. Once more, Brother Augustine and Brother Gregory play their guitars. Once more, the monks sing. Brother John holds up the bread, then the cups filled with wine.

When the monks pause in their singing, they and those assembled say the Lord's Prayer. A moment later there is the kiss of peace. The monks embrace each other. Those congregated shake hands, embrace, kiss, or engage in some other sign of joy and affection.

It is time for Communion, and a few of the monks stand at strategic places to distribute the small pieces of broken bread and the cups of wine. Virtually every man, woman, and child there stands in line to partake of Communion. When all have done so, the Mass is concluded. The monks walk back to the Priory for their midday meal, some stopping to mingle with friends and newcomers. Many of the visitors stay to picnic by the side of a pond next to the Priory.

I sit between Brother John and Brother Gregory at one of the long tables in the brick-floor dining room. The midday meal on Sundays is an occasion on which conversation is allowed throughout the meal. The food had been set out on a side table, and the monks and their invited guests have served themselves before sitting down.

"I'm amazed at how many people there were at the celebration of the Eucharist," I say to the prior.

"That's the usual number on Sundays during the summer," he responds. "Some people drive as long as seven to eight hours to get here. They will leave on Saturday, stay in a nearby hotel or motel, and then leave for home on Sunday afternoon."

For some years now, the liturgy, particularly the celebration of the Eucharist on Sunday, at Weston Priory (a few miles from the village of Weston in Vermont) has become a mecca for thousands of Catholics and non-Catholics. Part of this is due, no doubt, to the growing reputation of the monks at Weston Priory for their liturgical music, which is written by Brother Gregory and sung by the monks. The production of seven popular albums of this music has served to spread the knowledge of these talented Benedictine monks far and wide.

But as I discovered during my stay at Weston, this popularity is not just due to their being "the Singing Monks." Forged over the past decade and a half in a crucible of post-conciliar change, the Priory has developed a monastic community that could have far-reaching effects on both monasticism and on Roman Catholic spirituality.

My sojourn at Weston Priory had begun a few days earlier. An eight-seat airplane had brought me from Boston to Rutland, Vermont, where Brother Lawrence and Brother Ronald were waiting to drive me the fifteen-mile distance to the Priory. There, the guestmaster, Brother Richard, showed me to a small, delightful room in the guest house. It was late, and I went immediately to bed.

The next morning I was awakened by the ringing of bells. I looked at my watch: it was 4:45. Quickly I dressed and went downstairs to the room called the "Franklin room" (because it contains a Franklin stove), where the monks had gathered for morning vigil prayer.

The seventeen monks of Weston Priory were seated against the walls of the room, cross-legged and in the lotus position, on cushions. The vigil prayer began at 5 A.M. The brothers chanted two or three psalms, interspersed with readings from theology and the Gospel of the day, sang a song, listened to James Taylor's

"Fire and Rain," and spent a few moments in silent meditation. Another psalm was chanted, and then the monks departed.

The following two hours of the schedule at the Priory is a "quiet time." The monks eat breakfast during this time. It is not a meal in common: the brothers go in at any time during this period for breakfast. The rest of the two hours is spent in personal prayer.

I go into the dining room after vigil prayer. In silence I eat my breakfast and watch the dawn break over the Green Mountains.

After eating, I return to my room upstairs. It is small but cheerful, and looks out over a pond and part of the Green Mountain range. White walls, dark wood trim, and a broad-plank pine floor give it the appearance of a garret in a European hotel. I spend about three hours reading and writing, occasionally looking at the pastoral view out of my window.

At 9 A.M., Brother Richard knocks on my door. He informs me that three of the monks are waiting for me in the monastery's library.

Weston Priory's buildings are a complex of connected structures of different ages. The guest house is in the original early nineteenth-century farmhouse. Connected to this building is a chapel, a series of offices, and a long modern building that contains the rooms of the monks. Other buildings clustered around this complex are used as workshops.

Brother Richard guides me through the maze of corridors and down a flight of stairs, through a series of rooms, down another corridor, to the library, where I am introduced to Brother Elias and Brother Robert. Brother Lawrence, who is also there, I had already met. All three monks are attired in slacks and sport shirts, and I learn that the monks no longer wear habits. "We wear our cowls for certain liturgical functions," says Brother Elias, "but we generally wear what we have on now. St. Benedict, in the *Rule*, says that monks should wear the simple garb of the people; and we feel this makes more sense than wearing institutionalized clothes because centuries ago they were the 'garb of the people.' "

The four monks with whom I am conversing represent the wide range of backgrounds of those who are members of the community at Weston: Brother Richard had been a diocesan priest in New Jersey; Brother Robert had been a partner in a New York Stock Exchange firm; Brother Elias had spent some time in a Cistercian monastery; and Brother Lawrence had studied rare book restoration and worked at the Boston Public Library and for Harvard University.

Weston Priory had been mentioned extensively in *Turning East*,[1] the charming extended essay by theologian Harvey Cox, as having established a sense of community comparable to what the Buddhists call "sangha"; and our conversation turns to the essence of community in a monastic foundation.

"I would say that our community is based upon Gospel values lived out in deep personal commitment to God and to one another," Brother Elias begins. "The word *brother* is expressive, for us, of this choice to live as committed and caring persons, I believe."

"Brother" is key to the quality of community commitment at Weston Priory, and supersedes all other differences. There are several priests who are members of the community, but they are never addressed as "father." Except for noticing which of the priests is designated to consecrate the bread and wine at the celebration of the Eucharist, I find it impossible to tell who is ordained and who isn't. But the elimination of the distinction between priest and non-priest in nonliturgical aspects of monastic life at Weston is only the beginning of building community at the Priory.

"The Priory and its life is the collective responsibility of all the monks," says Brother Robert. "We all meet once or twice a day and decide on day-to-day matters, on longer-term policy, and share our joys and sorrows, our triumphs and our troubles, with each other. We have a prior, Brother John, but he does not play the 'father role,' which is what the abbot or prior traditionally was—the juridical head of the monastery. Instead, at Weston, authority resides in the community, and our decisions are made by finding consensus. The service asked of the prior is to assist the community in choosing a course of action in which we can all be of one heart and spirit."

The process by which Weston Priory achieved its innovative sense of community began in 1953 with its founding by a German Benedictine who was the abbot of the Monastery of the Abbey of

1. Harvey Cox, *Turning East: The Promise and the Peril of the New Orientalism* (New York: Simon & Schuster, 1977).

the Dormition in Jerusalem, the Abbot Leo Rudloff. The abbot spend most of the year in Jerusalem and the remainder at Weston, until 1969, when he retired. Since then, he has been a member of the community at Weston Priory (which became an independent monastic foundation in 1968) as Brother Leo.

The monks at Weston attribute the unusual characteristics of their monastery to Brother Leo's injunction when he was superior that they all should be "open to the Holy Spirit." It was the response to this inspiration or urging that caused the gradual change in Weston Priory from a traditional Benedictine foundation of strict observance to the unique monastic community that it is today, living the *Rule* of St. Benedict and responsive to the spirit of the times.

The monks at Weston Priory express the joy of community in a liturgical dance during mass. (Photo © 1978, The Benedictine Foundation of the State of Vermont, Inc.)

"There were some very fortuitous circumstances that helped along the way," Brother Lawrence says. "The Second Vatican Council, for all the pain of ferment and change that it brought, opened up monastic communities to renewal. And that, certainly, was a factor at Weston. But it was in the mid-1960s, when the community asked Brother John to be the prior, that change really began to take place.

"Brother John agreed to be the prior, but he made this conditional on certain factors: mainly, that there would be shared responsibility and communal decision-making; this would be the direction for our future growth as community." So this is the internal force that has shaped the Weston community within the Benedictine tradition.

I was to discover during the days that followed how unique and distinctive, how radical, the monastic community at Weston is: not only in its approach to monastic spirituality, but in its sense of community. What had been described to me in theoretical terms became more and more evident in reality: the love of the monks, one for the other, at Weston Priory was not just a commonplace, but was a vital, living presence.

"Then are they truly monks," St. Benedict observed, "when they live by the labor of their hands." Since the time from 8:30 A.M. to noon is a work period for the monks, the quartet of brothers volunteered to show me the workshops at the Priory.

The monks at Weston have evolved a format of work and prayer that is both innovative and suitable for them. The community, in its early years, supported itself by dairy farming and by agriculture. And, like all Vermonters, they made maple syrup in the spring. A new philosophy of work has emerged since then: the encouraging of each monk to develop those gifts expressive of one another. It is an approach to work based on a recognition of gifts rather than convention—an approach that has created an economy which is both diversified and stable, creative and personal.

"We made a decision some time ago," says Brother Richard, "to live entirely by our own work. Our individual labors make the community self-sufficient. People continue to offer us gifts, and this money is used for improving and extending facilities for our guests and visitors; for example, the roof adjacent to the hay barn, which allowed us to accommodate more persons for the Eucharist, and the Visitors' Center for the accommodation of guests who come here."

The first workshop we visit is that of Brother Lawrence. Trained as a book restorer and conservator, Brother Lawrence apprenticed as a hand bookbinder as well. Several libraries, including Harvard's, where he worked before coming to Weston Priory in 1970, continue to employ his skills.

Book presses, scraps of leather, knives, and the various implements of Brother Lawrence's bookbinding and book restoring trade are in evidence about his workshop. He shows me some of the work he is doing: the making of a case for a rare, fragile pamphlet of the seventeenth century; a leather binding for an eighteenth-century French illustrated book; the soaking in a special solution of some badly foxed pages of a nineteenth-century book.

We go out of the principal Priory building and walk along the edge of the pond to a small wooden building. Here, Brother Thomas is bending over a potter's wheel, intently fashioning a pot with his facile fingers. An accountant before he became a monk, Brother Thomas now creates pottery that is eagerly sought after by collectors.

"I'm sorry I have so few things to show you," says Brother Thomas, "but virtually everything is sold as soon as it comes out of the kiln."

The monks at Weston Priory are proud of Brother Thomas's work. The few pieces available for me to see are exquisite: the glaze, which is Brother Thomas's specialty, gives each piece a resemblance to blown glass. Brother Thomas began seriously to pursue his interest in pottery when he first came to Weston. He produced the usual ashtrays and mugs for the Priory giftshop. As his expertise and artistry grew, fewer and fewer purely utilitarian pieces were produced; today almost all of Brother Thomas's work is of an artistic nature, sought after by collectors and friends.

I look at the large bowls, vases, plates, and cups that Brother Thomas has produced. The exquisite design of each is highlighted by the extraordinary veneer of the glaze—a re-creation and development of ancient Chinese pottery glazing that Brother Thomas has skillfully mastered.

We leave the pottery workshop for another, similar building. Here, we see the work of Brother Richard and Brother Philip, two monks who work at graphic art, primarily silk-screening. In a building adjacent to the graphic art workshop is a room where Brother Elias works at cloisonné enameling.

I had noticed numerous photographs on the Priory's walls, and asked Brother Richard about them. "That's Brother Andrew's photography," he informs me. "Brother has developed this gift since he has been a monk. And the photographs sell in our giftshop."

Such creative occupations are not the only work that goes on at Weston Priory. Although the Priory has lessened the traditional importance of agriculture in monasteries, the cultivation of a garden for the needs of the Priory continues. And a number of the monks are engaged in a variety of forestry projects on the more than two hundred acres of woods that belong to the monastery. Caring for these woodlands reflects the community's environmental concern as well as providing fuel for heating the buildings during the long Vermont winters. In addition, some of the monks work at various clerical and bookkeeping tasks.

There is almost a medieval spirit of anonymous cooperation among the monks at Weston Priory in their discussion of the work done by each of them. Each is supportive and encouraging of the work done by the others. "Each gift is part of the community," says Brother Elias, "and everyone in the community participates in that gift. And because all of us are so close, this spirit brings out the gifts of each individual."

One endeavor, however, is shared by all the members of the community of Weston Priory: music. Through their recordings and songbooks, the brothers' music has become part of the lives and prayer of thousands of persons throughout the United States, Canada, Australia, England, and other countries.

"Our music is an expression of our life and prayer together," says Brother Gregory. The monks had led me to a sun-filled room with a piano and various recording equipment, and had introduced me to a monk sitting at the piano, playing an occasional few notes, jotting down something on a piece of paper, and humming. Brother Gregory writes the lyrics and music sung and recorded by the Weston monks.

"It all began during the time when we were shifting from Latin to English in the liturgy," says Brother Gregory. "None of us was satisfied with the music available to us at that time. One day I wrote a song, and the brothers liked it and sang it. I then wrote some more, and pretty soon we were all singing these songs during the Eucharist and for the Divine Office.

"Then people who heard us began telling us that we should share our music with those who couldn't come to the Priory to hear it, and that led us to print sheet music and songbooks with the music and to record our first album, 'Locusts and Wild Honey,' in 1971. We're now working on our eighth album."

The music of the Weston monks can perhaps be described as "modern Gregorian." It is reflective and expresses a solemn joy, characteristic of Gregorian chant, easily sung and yet contemporary in mood.

Each monk is involved in every aspect of the distinctive Weston music. Every monk sings it; every monk participates in recording it (which is done at the Priory); and every monk is involved in the details of filling the orders for records and songbooks.

The monastery bell rings, summoning us to the midday meal. Brother Gregory and I walk along the corridors to the dining room. The monks have set out the food on a long table, and we each serve ourselves and then stand at our places at the tables. When everyone is situated, one of the brothers begins a song of thanksgiving. We sit down after we have finished singing, and eat in silence, listening to Brother Peter read from Sheila Cassidy's gripping account of her life in Chile.

Brother John looks up, sees that everyone has almost finished eating, and rings a bell. The reading stops, and the monks quietly converse for a few moments. Then they begin to drift away, bringing their dishes into the kitchen, washing them and putting them away.

At 1:30 P.M., the monastery bell rings again. It is time for midday prayer, when the monks gather together to chant the Divine Office again. This time they use the chapel—a long room with a wooden table for an altar, a stone floor, and benches along the sides of the sanctuary. Along these benches the monks line up, facing each other, and alternate the chanting of the psalms. In fifteen or twenty minutes the prayers end, and the monks go off to their afternoon work.

I meet with Brother John, Brother Placid, and Brother Philip in the "Franklin room." I wish to pursue with the monks their distinctive sense of community and to hear about the process by which it came about.

"I hope you don't get the idea that this is some sort of psychological process," says Brother Placid. His bright smile and curly hair give him a cherubic look. "We don't have encounter groups here or bring in psychologists to tell us how to relate. You've probably heard this before, but we attribute our thoughts on the formation of the community to Brother Leo's always telling us to be open to the Holy Spirit. What this has meant for us is that we strive to become more totally alive and free."

"You can see this in our work," adds Brother Philip. "Each of us endeavors to bring out special gifts in the others. What's important is not what gifts we came here with, but how, within the context of the community, we develop these gifts and perhaps discover latent gifts. Brother Thomas hadn't developed his pottery gift before coming to Weston, nor Brother Andrew and Brother Gregory their respective gifts in photography and music."

Brother John explains one of the methods by which the monks of Weston Priory achieve their high degree of sensitivity to each other. "If you're open to the Holy Spirit," he begins, "you're also open to each other. The question we always ask ourselves is: 'How can we most genuinely be a Christian community, a Gospel community?' Well, out of this comes the conclusion that we must love one another as Jesus loves us. We've all heard this before, but how do we make it a reality?

"We have a chapter meeting each morning to discuss day-to-day business, longer-range policy, what's been happening with each of us. Then, every month we have a retreat for three days. During this time we don't have guests, don't celebrate the liturgy or the Divine Office for the public, but spend a great deal of time in personal and community sharing with each other on value topics. This sharing is given a high priority in our community life. And at any time, one of the brothers may want to get two or three others together to discuss some problem, some joy, or to work out some troublesome thought."

"It's important that we always know what is essential to our life together," continues Brother Philip. "The sacramental value of our life is in our witness as a comunity rooted in the Word of God."

Despite what may seem to be exclusivity, the monks of Weston Priory have an outreach that encompasses thousands. Weekends during the summer and fall see from 700 to 1,000 persons coming to the Priory for the celebration of the Eucharist and to participate with the monks in the chanting of the Divine Office. Smaller numbers come to share quietly throughout the weekdays of the year in the daily Eucharist and other times of prayer, or for brief periods as guests in the monastery's guest houses, where they share meals, work, and reflection with the monks, thus sharing more fully the life of the community.

"Our life is so blessed that we want to share the overflow," says Brother Placid. "And that's why we share with others. It isn't just the liturgy that we share with those who come here, it's our witness to community: to the fact that relationships can endure, that people can be creative together, and to the reality of the Gospels."

The monastery bell rings once again. It is 4:30 P.M., and the bell signals the end of the afternoon work period. The monks now come in from their tasks, shower, and prepare for the 5:15 P.M. celebration of the Eucharist, which will take place in the chapel.

The three monks and I chat some more about Weston's spirit of community, and then go to the chapel.

Supper follows the celebration of the Eucharist; and the meal is followed by the chanting of Compline at 7 P.M.

A stillness descends on Weston Priory after Compline. It is the time of the "great silence" in monasteries. Crickets and frogs punctuate this stillness with their rhythmical dissonance. A few of the monks take solitary strolls before going to bed; others go to their rooms to read or pray.

Silence is of great moment in monastic communities. At Weston, silence has a positive value. "It is a time when we listen to God and to ourselves," Brother Elias had said to me earlier in the day. "But silence is also when we listen carefully to one of our brothers."

The grey predawn light and the 4:45 A.M. bell simultaneously awaken me the next morning. Once again I hurriedly dress and wash, and go to the "Franklin room" for vigil prayer. I smile as I look at the monks sitting on cushions, waiting to begin this first common prayer of the day, and I remember Brother John relating the experience of how the present form of their Vigil had evolved.

"Most of us had lost enthusiasm for the previous vigil form with its several chanted psalms and traditional readings at 4 A.M. We then felt we would like to try integrating some more contemporary elements with regard to content, place, and dress. Zen cushions, clothing of one's own choice, and elements such as current theological readings, recorded folk songs, and poems and psalms were experimented with until we evolved satisfactory elements which brought us to the point where we felt we were *celebrating* the wonderful time of the day which early morning is."

Brother Robert, a former partner in a New York investment banking firm, now bakes bread at Weston Priory. (Photo © 1978, The Benedictine Foundation of the State of Vermont, Inc.)

The sitting on cushions in the yoga position is yet another example of the monks of Weston Priory being open to divergent religious traditions. Someone friendly to the monastery had given the monks the cushions and had instructed them in hatha yoga. "We have had some instruction in yoga, Zen meditation, and other spiritual disciplines," Brother Elias had said to me, "but we look on these as techniques, as aids to prayer. Our prayer can probably be best described as scripture-centered. Prayer for us is also an aspect of our relationship to each other."

The sun begins to stream into the dining room as I eat breakfast. Mist is rising from the pond as if it were an offering for the newly beginning day. After finishing my corn flakes and coffee, I wash my dishes and go to my room to spend a few hours writing. At 9 A.M., Brother Richard knocks at my door once more to tell me that Brother John, Brother Placid, and Brother Elias are available if I wish to speak with them. I make my way to the monastic library, where the three monks have gathered.

Because it had been on my mind since vigil prayer that morning, I begin our discussion by asking about the prayer life of the community.

"One of the unusual aspects of prayer and worship which we have explored," begins Brother Placid, "is the area of dance. A friend of ours—George Young—was quite knowledgeable in dance of all kinds, and he is the one who began to teach us. At first, this was just for recreation. And then we began to incorporate it into the liturgy.

"There were a lot of factors that went into this: our dancing together was a particularly joyful way of expressing our lives together; it has a Biblical inspiration in King David dancing in front of the Ark of the Covenant; and we have also been inspired by our contact with Shakers, who, as you know, use dance as part of their act of worship."

Brother Elias got up and brought me a photograph taken by Brother Andrew that had been hanging on the wall of the corridor outside the library. The photograph showed the monks holding hands in a large circle in the hay barn—the shining sun almost making their light grey cowls transparent. The spirit of lilting joy was evident in the striking picture.

"One woman told us that she found our dancing at the Eucharist made her uncomfortable," Brother John says, flashing a broad smile. "But she also said that she didn't want us to stop."

The continuous unfolding of the Weston monks' "joyful seizing of life" now comes forth also in their interpretation of their vows. "St. Benedict says that the vows are stability, conversion of life, and obedience," says Brother Elias. "Traditionally, stability meant that you were committed to the monastery that you had chosen—to the place. Well, we interpret stability as commitment to each other.

"We understand conversion to life as freeing ourselves in the Gospel spirit so that we become able to give and receive in simplicity and truth.

"And obedience, for us, means attentive listening, willingness to dialogue."

For all the closeness of the monks of Weston Priory, they are open to participating in the world at large. Their concern for the rehabilitation of war-torn Vietnam resulted in their producing a 45 r.p.m. record and donating all the proceeds from its sale to a fund for Vietnamese rehabilitation established by the American Friends Service Committee. The appeal by friends on behalf of the Moskitos, a group of Indians living in the northeastern part of Honduras with their own language, customs, and traditions, led to the monks at Weston helping to produce an album of the music of the Moskitos. And the proposal by other friends that they become involved in the antinuclear movement led them, after a great deal of dialoguing, to go to New York to participate in "The Mobilization for Human Survival," a religious convocation. At the Stephen Weiss Free Synagogue, where the day's activities ended, the monks followed Alan Ginsberg, who read a poem by Lawrence Ferlinghetti. Their contribution to this antinuclear protest was to dance.

Causes are not the only outreach of the community. On different occasions they have visited the remaining Shaker community in Maine and a Sufi community in New York; and the Priory itself has received many guests from communities throughout the United States.

The ringing of bells once more ends our conversation and calls us to the midday meal and then to prayer. The four of us gather again in the library in the early afternoon.

"What process do you use to integrate any new persons into the community?" I ask to begin our new session.

"If someone feels that he wishes to become a monk at Weston," Brother John says, "we ask him to get to know each of the brothers and to spend about a year making long visits here. If, after that time, he still wishes to become a member of the community, and the brothers agree that he should be accepted, then he becomes what we call a 'new brother.' This would be comparable to the period of postulancy and novitiate in most religious communities."

"If after several years of integration, the community and the new brother decide that they are at a point where their knowledge and love for one another have matured," Brother John continues, "then we celebrate this with his solemn profession of vows."

"What strikes us," says Brother Placid, "about this way of integrating new brothers is that it is experienced as a spirit of passage into community life, rather than a fixed process."

The monastic calling is the prophetic one of creative vision and witness. In the words of Brother John:

> For us, the newness of monastic expression is firmly grounded in our ancient religious tradition—even as the newness of liturgical expression or the newness of theological expression since Vatican II are grounded in scriptural inspiration and ecclesiastical tradition.
>
> The ground of prophetic life in the Church is clearly affirmed in Paul's letters when he describes the church as "founded on the prophets and apostles."
>
> The vocation to prophetic life in both the Old and New Testaments embodies a twofold gift: the gift of VISION and the gift of CREATIVE WITNESS TO THAT GIFT OF VISION. While the prophetic vocation is chiefly manifest in chosen individuals in Israel, the same calling is often seen as a community gift among the followers of Jesus.
>
> The gift of vision is a special way of seeing. It involves seeing creation and humanity from the viewpoint of Jesus. It is rooted in prayerful reflection, in communion with God.
>
> The gift of vision is concerned with the actual human condition, with its pain and its possibilities, its sinfulness and its holiness, its hopes and its fear, with its living and its dying.
>
> The gift of creative witness has to do with communication of that vision, with the living out in a visible way what is seen by the prophetic community as the reality and the alternatives offered in the Spirit of Jesus.

As the brothers at Weston have grown in their awareness of this monastic vocation, certain signs of the times have emerged as significant for Gospel witness.

Through openness to the world around them, they have tried to recognize these signs of the times and to respond to them. The loneliness of so many people, the many signs of alienation and violence in society, the dissatisfaction with personal relationships, with work and with play, the need to escape from reality—all these have spoken of the pain and the destructiveness which face humanity in our times.

It is because of such signs that the life of the community at Weston is focused on hospitality, on the depth and faithfulness of personal relationships, on the qualities of gentleness, care, and concern for others, on the centrality of forgiveness, openness, and prayerful silence.

In a society where conversation on batting averages and hockey scores forms the easiest mode of communication and friendship, and where the topics of human rights, nuclear proliferation, death, and dying cannot be addressed, a witness to deeper levels of communication and communion among people is a human necessity.

In a society where the value of work is measured by dollars, hours, and numbers rather than the giftedness of the worker, the needs and dignity of the person, a witness to creativity, personal expression, care, and concern is a vital need.

In a society where unity is seen as conformity, as the result of abnegation of personal responsibility, as the achievement of force and compulsion, there is a need for the witness to a unity achieved through free choice, through the inspiration of authentic leadership and inspiration.

It is out of such a vision and such a challenge to creativity that the present form of monastic life at Weston has been realized.

The brothers recognize this form as being provisional; it must constantly be evaluated in light of the changing signs of the times.

But it is also stable and dependable, for its strength and endurance is based on a firm choice in faith and love: the commitment to one another in the Spirit of Jesus and his Gospel, within a communal way of life as lived by Benedict and his followers.

In the course of history, much of this vision has been enriched and much has been lost. It is the challenge of the new monasticism to sift out this history and to build a new prophetic witness on a firm foundation.

Perhaps the most significant element which has become blurred in the course of history is the propetic vision and witness itself.

For monastic characteristics have often become absorbed in the development—both legitimate and necessary—of more modern religious communities. These communities are service-oriented, destined to assist the pastoral mission of the church; works of education, preaching, and sacramental ministry.

The monastic calling is one of creative vision and witness, often a challenge and a counterwitness to church, church authority, society, and accepted mores.

"How is it that everything sounds so good?" I ask. "In the days that I've been here, I've been amazed at the nurturing and love that each of you exhibits towards each other. Is it really that simple?"

The three monks chortle. "There is a woman who visits from time to time and who once told us that the trouble with us is that we're too happy and too joyful," says Brother Elias. " 'Where is your suffering?' she would ask us. Well, as with any family, any community, there are problems, there is growth and change, which sometimes can have painful aspects, but it is our commitment to each other, our willingness always to share our lives together that transcends these problems. Each of us knows that we feel our brokenness, but we also feel our joy much more."

"Our challenge is the prophecy of hope and joy," says Brother John. "We've chosen to celebrate life."

In my days at Weston Priory, I witnessed more and more the reality of this community of monks—a reality that was beyond words. In the monastic witness of this small group, tucked away in Vermont's Green Mountains, was the basis for the spirit of community and relationships in our contemporary society. For the person who wished to observe what "loving one another" (or, "relating to each other," to use the terminology of humanistic psychology) meant, the experience of Weston Priory would give that person a vision of reality.

It was perhaps symbolical that on the day I left, immediately after the celebration of the Eucharist, the monks were singing one of their songs that touched on this prophetic vision:

> Wherever you go I shall go.
>
> Wherever you live so shall I live.
>
> Your people will be my people, and
> your God will be my God, too.
>
> Wherever you die, I shall die, and
> there I shall be buried beside you.
>
> We will be together forever, and
> our love will be the gift of our
> life.
>
> . . . .
> The color and texture which you have
> brought into my being
>
> Have become a song and I want to
> sing it forever.
>
> There is an energy in us
> which makes things happen
> when the paths of other persons
> touch ours, and we have to be
> there to let it happen. . . .*

* From the album "Wherever You go," copyright 1972 by The Benedictine Foundation of the State of Vermont, Inc. Author and composer: Gregory Norbet, O.S.B., Weston Priory.

7

The Holy Order of MANS

THE tall young man who greets me at the door of the Victorian building near San Francisco's Haight-Ashbury district flashes a smile of welcome.

"Hello, I'm Brother Fred Crowley. We've been expecting you. Please follow me."

The first signs of dawn are appearing as I walk down a flight of stairs to a chapel where about forty men and women, attired in dress similar to that worn by Roman Catholic priests and nuns, are waiting for the daily communion, or mass, to begin. It is 6:15 A.M. The members of the Holy Order of MANS had arisen at 5:30 A.M., had already spent fifteen minutes in meditation in common, and are now engaged in the daily eucharistic celebration that begins each day.

When the communion service has ended, Brother Fred escorts me upstairs for breakfast. The dining room is filled with men and women—mostly in their twenties and thirties—wearing blue clerical garb with "Roman" collars and a cross, or blue dresses, also with clerical collars. Breakfast is finished at about 7:30 A.M., and the dining room clears as the men and women begin their workday.

My guide leads me up another flight of stairs to the book-lined study of Father Vincent Rossi, the Director General of the Holy Order of MANS, who patiently tells me about the origins of this distinctive, nondenominational religious order. Aside from the identification as "Christian," and rites, practices, and doctrine reminiscent of Roman Catholicism, the Holy Order of MANS is not a religion, although its priests—both men and women—do serve as pastors or spiritual directors to groups who form Christian churches—again, nondenominational. And the Order's priests do celebrate a mass and dispense various sacraments.

"We were founded in 1968 here in San Francisco," Father Rossi tells me. "The Holy Order of MANS was the result of some thirty years of preliminary work of, and revelation to, the late Father Paul Blighton. Born out of revelation, the Order has its roots in the living presence of Jesus Christ as the living Word for this present age. The Order also uses the ancient wisdom teachings, and in particular the writings of Paul the Apostle, who in the first century of Christianity worked to unify all churches."

From Father Rossi, I learn the basic facts about the Holy Order of MANS (which stands for four Greek words: *mysterion*, *agape*, *nous*, and *sophia*). There are now six hundred persons under life vows, about three hundred more in training, and over a thousand in Christian communities as lay adherents. Many more are enrolled in the Discipleship program, a correspondence course. There are sixty centers of the Holy Order of MANS in the United States and several in foreign countries. The main center for the Order is this one in San Francisco (although the administrative headquarters are located on a farm and retreat center north of San Francisco). Virtually all of the members of the Order work at outside jobs, Father Rossi tells me, in an imitation of St. Paul, who supported himself and his missionary activities by following his occupation as a tentmaker. Income from these jobs is turned over to the Order. No donations or outside funds are accepted, and no member of the Order receives a salary.

We move on to the theological basis for the Order, when we are interrupted by a knock at the door. Father Rossi introduces me to Sister Christine Olson, who brings a tray containing a pot of coffee, two cups and saucers, and some rolls.

"The Order claims no theology of its own," Father Rossi says, after he has poured each of us a cup of coffee and handed me a sweet roll. "The doctrinal foundation of the Order rests on the basic doctrines of the Christian tradition, namely the triune God and the divinity of Christ. Since the Order teaches a path of Christian mysticism, and since there could be no Christian mysticism without the Incarnate Word and the Trinity of Persons in the unity of the Divine Nature, these doctrines are fundamental.

"The Order also accepts the authority of the Bible as divine revelation. To ask what is the theological basis of the Holy Order of MANS is like asking what is the theological basis of the Dominicans or the Franciscans. They have no theology of themselves as an Order, but only in so far as they partake of the Christian traditions through the Church.

"In the Order, the emphasis is not placed on precision of theological expression nor on the novelty of doctrine, but rather on spiritual method. This is to say the flavor of the Order's teaching is more metaphysical and mystical than it is theological. In fact, the Order has little in common with the tendencies of modern Christian theology; the spirit of the Order feels much more at home with traditional Christian teaching in its best and highest sense, as exemplified by such saints and mystics as Clement of Alexandria, Gregory of Nyssa, Pseudo-Dionysius the Areopagite, St. Bernard of Clairvaux, St. Francis of Assisi, St. Thomas Aquinas, Meister Eckhart, St. Theresa of Avila, St. John of the Cross, and Jacob Boehme.

"The path to spiritual realization or to mystical union is fraught with many dangers for the individual. This is why it is necessary to have a solid foundation in scriptural authority and sound doctrine. Since these doctrines stem from the original Revelation, they provide, as it were, infallible guides for the individual soul as he travels the path toward union with God.

"Modern theology, in its effort to be 'up to date,' has almost completely lost sight of the indispensable value of its ancient tradition, based as it is on primordial and unchanging Truth."

I am struck, as Father Rossi finishes his discourse, at how the Holy Order of MANS has cut through almost two thousand years of Christian theological development and controversy, and has re-established the simple "societies of friends," with their elementary credal beliefs and sense of the immanence of Jesus, which characterized primitive Christianity.

Father Rossi excuses himself to go to another appointment; but I remain in his study to talk with Brother Fred Crowley, who had escorted me around the house earlier in the day. Father Rossi had asked him to talk with me about his experience with the Holy Order of MANS; and I now turn my attention to this genial member of the Order.

Brother Fred is one of the small minority of the Holy Order of MANS who does not have an outside job: he is an accountant in the treasurer's office. From Connecticut, of an Irish-Catholic background, he tells me that he was devout in his boyhood and had strong religious feelings, but could find no outlet for them in the Roman Catholicism that he experienced. It was while he was attending the University of Connecticut, and was desirous of changing his life, that someone told him about the Holy Order of MANS. In 1974, at the age of twenty-two, he entered the Order.

The training that Fred Crowley underwent is standard for all those who wish to become members of the Holy Order of MANS. An applicant must first be approved by the Esoteric Council—the governing body of the Order—to begin a novitiate training. After three months under a vow of obedience, the trainee appears before a regional council for an interview and takes temporary vows. The candidate now begins a year of training in philosophy, Bible studies, and self-development.

Following this year, the candidate moves on to a missionary training program and serves a year in one of the two sub-orders of the Holy Order of MANS—either the Brown Brothers of the Holy Light (males) or the Immaculate Heart Sisters of Mary (females). During this year, a vow of celibacy is added to the temporary vows. This period is oriented around selfless service. At the end of the year, life vows are administered—vows of service, humility, obedience, poverty, and purity. And, following the taking of vows, two years of "on-the-job" training in Order-related programs are required.

Upon application to the Esoteric Council, the members of the Order may be admitted to advanced training for ministry. This advanced training completed, they may become either priests or ministers.

The service work of the Holy Order of MANS is diverse and ranges from youth hostels and women's aid facilities to street missionary work. Members of the Order who hold outside jobs must also participate in this service work during hours when they aren't working or studying.

A bell rings in the house, and Brother Fred Crowley tells me that it is time for midday meditation. We descend two flights of stairs and go once more into the chapel, where those members of the Order who work in the house are gathering for a half-hour of meditation. (Those who work at outside jobs may meditate as part of their luncheon periods, if practical, or are "mindful" of the period of meditation if their schedules don't permit formal meditation.)

Two members of the Holy Order of MANS arrange a growing library at the Order's Raphael House.

At noon, another bell announces that lunch is being served, and we file up to the dining room for the midday meal. I sit at a table with Brother Fred and Sister Christine Olson.

Sister Christine was raised in Oregon and Washington. Like Brother Fred, she was raised a Roman Catholic. While attending the University of Portland and the University of Oregon, majoring in the social sciences, she began to read about Eastern spiritual practices and to become involved in social causes.

"I was very conscious of looking for a spiritual community and for a vehicle for service to others," she says. "I couldn't find these things in Catholicism, and the aspect of a spiritual community was lacking in social service agencies.

"One day I was sitting in a coffee shop in Portland run by the Holy Order of MANS called the Wheel of Fortune when a woman dressed like a nun came in and sat next to me. She told me that she was a priest with the Holy Order of MANS and invited me to hear a lecture at the Order's center in Portland. I wasn't very enthusiastic about going; but I was curious and did go. I was impressed and intrigued. After getting to know the Order better, I decided to enter. It has not only fulfilled my earlier aspirations, but has fulfilled my life."

Sister Christine is dressed in a light blue robe with a white "Roman" collar. A cross dangles from her neck. In her late twenties, with short blond hair, Sister Christine works as a secretary in the house. In the evening she does street missionary work in San Francisco's tough Tenderloin district — a section filled with pimps and prostitutes, young male hustlers, transvestites, alcoholics, and the destitute elderly.

"We go in teams of two," Sister Christine informs me, "one man and one woman. We don't do any preaching. We just walk. If anyone wants help or just wants to talk to us, we're available."

I ask her about the Order's policy on dating, and she smiles shyly. "It's rare to have someone date or marry someone who's not in the Order," she says. "But there are no rules against it. There isn't much time for dating — most of us mingle with whomever happens to be living in the house where we are stationed. But if we find that we're attracted to someone in particular and want to spend more time with that one person, then we get the permission of our superior for what we call 'courting' or 'keeping company' — quaint words, aren't they? And if this courtship should lead to a desire to marry, the Esoteric Council has to sanction the engagement."

Both Brother Fred and Sister Christine are in stages of advanced training in the Holy Order of MANS; and both have indicated their desire to become ordained priests. (Men and women priests and ordained ministers of the Order are called "Reverend"; and those not ordained are called "Brother" or "Sister.") As with all members of the Order, they may be sent anywhere in the world. Sister Christine began in Portland, spent a short period in San Francisco, then Reno, Chicago, Erie, and St. Louis before returning to San Francisco. Brother Fred entered the Order in Boston and did missionary work in South Carolina and Arkansas before coming to San Francisco in 1976.

We rise from our table and proceed again to the chapel for another half-hour of meditation. At 1 P.M., my two companions go back to their respective jobs, and I go upstairs to talk with Father Rossi again.

Looking out of the window of his study, I see a building across the street with the sign "San Francisco Youth Hostel." In this turn-of-the-century converted building, the Holy Order of MANS operates a hostel, affiliated with the International Youth Hostel, one of five such facilities that the Order runs in the United States. Next to it, in a large park at the corner of the street, is yet another sign of the Order's service activities: through the efforts of the Order, this park, overrun with weeds and unsafe, has been cleaned up and made usable for the residents of the neighborhood. Up the street from it, a piece of vacant land owned by a church has been transformed into a playground for children.

There is a knock at the door: a red-robed man enters, seeking a book, followed by a woman in a light-blue robe who tells me that Father Rossi will be with me in a few moments. (I had learned that red robes are used by the Order's male priests when in the house, and that light-blue house robes are used by the women. Black clerical garb is used when outside of the house.)

Father Rossi enters, bearing two cups of coffee. We discuss the monastic aspects of the Holy Order of MANS. "We are dealing with new concepts of monasticism," he tells me, "of going from a brotherhouse into the world, so to speak, and back again into the brotherhouse. It is a blending of activity and contemplation. But we also recognize that different persons have different calls, and we have two sub-orders for those who are called to a life of more contemplation."

These sub-orders—the one for men called the Brown Brothers of the Holy Light and located in Detroit, the other for women called the Immaculate Heart Sisters of Mary and located in St. Louis—serve both as vehicles for those members of the Holy Order of MANS who are called to a life of greater contemplation and as part of the training for all members of the Order. The sub-orders, members of which are able to take vows that are renewable, include the element of celibacy. And the year that each member of the Order must spend in a sub-order includes celibacy.

"However," says Father Rossi, "this year of training does not apply to married couples who enter the Order. There is an alternate program for them."

Throughout my conversations with Father Rossi and other members of the Order, there is a strong insistence that "Jesus Christ is accepted as Master of the Order." The organizational structure, however, is vested in the Director General, an office now held by Father Rossi, and the Esoteric Council. This duality both governs the administration of the Order and oversees its spiritual development.

"There is another aspect of the Order," Father Rossi continues, "that is of importance: spiritual masters or teachers. There are seven of them, and we look upon them as having a sacramental function—much like the bishops of the early Church. The masters exist alongside the administrative hierarchy. They serve very much like the bishops and presbyters of primitive Christianity: to interpret the teachings of Christ, to lead persons into a greater union with God, to ordain, and so forth. A spiritual master is someone who, because of his own life and his advancement in understanding the truths of Scripture, is called by God to unveil these truths to others."

The Holy Order of MANS extends to two other religious aspects beyond its status as a religious order with men and women under vows: the Discipleship Movement and the Christian Community Movement. The first of these—the Discipleship Movement—is a lay order composed of members not under vows, but who have made an inner commitment to prepare and raise themselves spiritually.

This lay order extension is operated through a correspondence course system under an assigned Class Master to study Scripture and to learn the spiritual exercises of the Order.

"The Christian Community aspect of the Holy Order of MANS,

on the other hand," says Father Rossi, "is the development of a spiritual community, sponsored by the Order, composed of groups of people who have decided to participate as fully as possible in community life as a means to awaken the realization of God in their daily lives. A priest or minister of the Order serves as the pastor of such a Christian Community. I've made arrangements for you to meet Reverend Bob Harrison, who is pastor of the Christian Community of San Francisco."

It is already late afternoon when Father Rossi and I conclude our discussion. The house is bustling with activity as the workday comes to an end. Many of those who are working at outside jobs are returning. In just a short while, at 5 P.M., the members of the Order will gather in the chapel for an hour of meditation. Supper will be served at 6 P.M. From 7 P.M. to 10 P.M., the members of the Order will be engaged in a variety of activities: classes, individual study, and service work. At 10 P.M., they will gather for evening prayer; and from 10:30 to 11:00 P.M., for another half-hour of meditation. The hour before midnight is left them for any personal tasks and to prepare for the next day.

The former Golden Gate Hospital has been transformed by paint and minor construction work into Raphael House—a women's aid facility operated by the Holy Order of MANS in San Francisco. When I enter, the receptionist calls Brother John Robinson to tell him that I have arrived; and a few moments later the elevator door opens, and a dark-haired, clerically attired man greets me.

Brother John Robinson (an ordained minister in the Holy Order of MANS, who prefers to be addressed as "Brother") is in his early forties and has been a member of the Order since 1974. He had been raised in a devout Baptist home, but had converted to Catholicism. Following his divorce, he fell away from the Roman Catholic faith; but soon after, he again became a practicing Roman Catholic. His life before entering the Holy Order of MANS was spent as a successful actor and singer in the theatre.

"I guess my life changed when a fellow actor became ill with terminal cancer, a man whom I had known well for a long time," he tells me as we wait for the director of Raphael House in a small parlor on the second floor. "He became quite frightened as the result of his impending death, and I wanted to do all that I could to help him during the crisis. I had encountered the Order in both Pittsburgh and New York, and somehow had heard about a member of the Order in Boston who was known as a spiritual healer. I went to see him about my friend, and, in the process, went through a profound spiritual experience which led to my entering the Order."

The door of the parlor opens, and I am introduced by Brother John to an elderly woman with short, cropped white hair and twinkling blue-grey eyes. Her black dress, white "Roman" collar, and cross announce her as a member of the Holy Order of MANS, but she corrects me when I address her as "Sister."

"I was married for over fifty years, and I don't intend to drop my married name to be called 'Sister Ellen,' " she instructs me in a feisty but humorous way. "Call me Mrs. Rigney."

Ellen Rigney is eighty-five years of age. Her energy is a model for members of the Holy Order of MANS. Following her husband's death in 1962, she spent three years in the VISTA program, organizing day-care centers in North Carolina and Oregon. Then she moved to San Francisco, where she continued to be active in service work. She met the founder of the Holy Order of MANS, Father Paul Blighton, shortly after he founded the Order, and she offered him her volunteer services.

"He told me that it wasn't enough for me to offer my services," says Mrs. Rigney. "I had to live the life of the Order. Well, just after he died I did enter the Order. I was eighty-one years old; but I went through the training—just like everyone else."

The three of us leave the parlor to tour Raphael House. This women's aid facility provides shelter, food, clothing, counseling, referral, and many other related services for women, children, and families. There are about fifty beds in Raphael House; and the women who seek shelter there sign a three-day contract, which is mutually renewable. Thirty-two members of the Holy Order of MANS are involved in the facility: twelve of these work at outside jobs to provide funds to maintain the operation.

"The goal of Raphael House," Brother John informs me, "is to provide truly holistic service to the individual and the community. Its philosophy is that you cannot solve a problem in the community without answering the need in the individual that corresponds to the social problem. A problem in one human dimension is likely to reflect in all the others. The approach of those who work in Raphael House is to strive to make whole, to heal, to give comfort, to serve as best they can all the dimensions of the whole person."

Children are cared for at Raphael House by two members of the Holy Order of MANS.

We peek into a large room, decorated with the finger paintings of children, where a young woman member of the Order is telling stories to about a dozen children whose mothers are residing at Raphael House.

"This is the heart and spirit of Raphael House," Mrs. Rigney says to me as we enter the chapel. Austere but warm, the chapel contains an altar, candelabra, and flower-filled vases. The pews, Mrs. Rigney tells me, were a gift from a nearby Episcopalian church.

The former hospital rooms have been converted into simple, freshly painted rooms for the residents of Raphael House. A bed, a chair, and a chest of drawers furnish them. Occasionally a small bed or crib indicates that a child or children also occupy the room. Some of the larger rooms are used for entire families.

"Sometimes a woman comes to us because of marital problems," says Brother John. "Whenever possible, we like to have the husband join his wife and children and work out the problems here."

The cheerful, sparkling dining room is next on our tour. It looks out on a carefully attended garden next door. Flowers are arranged on each table in the dining room. Three brothers are working in the large kitchen, preparing the evening meal.

"Most residents come in with a hopeless feeling of 'Where do I go from here?'," says Brother John. "Actually, most want to find work; they don't want welfare, but life has been so hard, and they are now down so far, it seems impossible to rise up. One resident said, 'Unless you understand what it's like to be at the bottom of the barrel, it's hard to understand my situation.' We gave this woman enough time to work out her problems, and now both she and her husband and their baby are back together again. With God's help, we hope to help those who come to us find a footing again. We know we have with certain residents, and it is a most rewarding feeling."

Our final stop is at Brother Juniper's Coffee House, a just-opened facility on the ground floor of Raphael House. Like all else at Raphael House, Brother Juniper's is sparkling clean, attractively decorated, and bustling with the efficient cheerfulness of the members of the Holy Order of MANS who are working there.

Brother Juniper's was started, Mrs. Rigney tells me, as a fund-raising venture for Raphael House.

"It is also a much-needed place in the area for people to get some good food at a reasonable price," adds Brother John, "and to have a comfortable place to meet."

As I leave this hospice, I comment to Brother John and Mrs. Rigney on the cheerfulness, tranquility, and optimism that the members of the Order exhibited as I encountered them on my tour of Raphael House. I had noticed the same spirit at the center on Steiner Street.

"Do I have to tell you why?" asks Mrs. Rigney.

"No, I think it's obvious," I respond.

"God bless, and please come again," says Brother John as I depart.

"Hello, I'm the Reverend Bob Harrison," said the red-robed, mid-thirtyish, balding man who opened the door to the converted storefront. A sign announced this as the Christian Community Center of San Francisco. "Let me introduce you to my wife, Sister Martha."

Sister Martha Harrison, wearing a blue robe, was in the final throes of pregnancy with the couple's first child.

The Reverend Bob Harrison and I walked across the street to the Tassajara Bakery, where we purchased two cups of coffee, and walked back to the Center. The buildings of the Haight-Ashbury glistened in the early morning sun.

The three of us sat in a small office off the foyer of the Center. The Reverend Bob Harrison told me about being raised in San Francisco and adjacent Marin County, his involvement with the counterculture during the 1960s, and his use of drugs. Bob Harrison, like many of the members of the Holy Order of MANS whom I met, was raised a Roman Catholic.

"In 1968," he continues, "I had a converting experience: I had the memory that I had had a relationship with Jesus Christ in a past life. I was living in a commune at this time, and, because of God's Providence, I happened to meet Father Blighton. These events made me confront certain realities: that Jesus Christ is real, that I can have a real, intimate relationship with Him. In December, 1968, I joined the Holy Order of MANS."

Following his training and his living in various cities throughout the United States, the Reverend Bob Harrison became the pastor of the Christian Community of San Francisco. By that time he had married, and he and his wife now serve as joint pastors of the Christian Community.

The Christian Communities began as an outreach program of the Holy Order of MANS. During the early days of the Order, as missionaries were sent out to various cities in the United States to teach classes, give lectures, and hold services, many who had attended these classes and lectures joined in the discussions, attended prayers and services, and developed friendships with others there. The Order found that many people wanted to continue receiving the sacraments and attending classes. In response to this, it began to assign permanent ministers to those places that looked the most promising for community work.

As interest grew, core groups of persons committed to working together with the Order's ministers grew into permanent fellowships. A charter was prepared by the Order. If enough people could be found who were willing to commit 10 percent of their income to the development of a spiritual community in their area, the Order would send them a charter, granting them authority to operate as a Christian Community of the Holy Order of MANS. A member of the Order, trained in the spiritual ministry, would be sent to each such community. There are now some twenty such Christian communities in the United States.

"What has come into being," says the Reverend Bob Harrison, "is not a new religion, not a new philosophy, or a new theology, but rather a new form of organization within which a comprehensive teaching approach could coalesce—a form free of traditional associations, yet within the great Christian tradition; therefore free to evolve according to the direction of the Spirit and the needs of man."

Membership in a Christian Community is open to all those who willingly elect to follow its way of life. A ninety-day orientation period is required for all those who seek membership. During this time there are classes, lectures, and activities to prepare the individual for membership. Prospective members are introduced to the basic principles of a Christian Community (a document called "Tenets and Strivings"), learn about prayer and meditation, and observe how life is lived in a Christian Community. When the three-month orientation is fulfilled, the prospective member may then petition the governing board for full membership in the Community.

The eighty-five members of the Christian Community of San Francisco lead lives very much centered around this spiritual community. Each Sunday the communion service takes place at 11 A.M., and evening prayers commence at 9:30 P.M. The daily communion service is at 6 A.M. (7 A.M. on Saturdays). A board meeting takes place each Monday evening. On Tuesday, Wednesday, and Thursday evenings there are classes; and on Friday evenings there are occasionally special lectures or social events.

In addition, twelve members of the Community (including the Harrisons) live in apartments in the Haight-Ashbury building leased for the Christian Community's center.

In this building the Community also operates a school. Currently, the three teachers instruct eighteen students (half of these are children of members of the Christian Community) in grades kindergarten through third grade.

Sister Martha has left her husband and me to greet the members of the Community who have started to gather for this Sunday morning's communion service; and soon the Reverend Harrison excuses himself as well.

The sidewalk in front of the foyer and the foyer itself are filled with members of the Community who have gathered for the service. Some have already gone into the chapel, adjacent to the foyer, to pray or meditate. Most are young—in their twenties or thirties—and without exception they seem committed to their involvement in this religious community experience.

Roger Jacobs, a new member of the Christian Community, introduces himself to me. Jacobs, in his late twenties, is from Kentucky. He tells me that he majored in philosophy and literature in college, and that he enjoys reading, classical music, traveling, and camping. Currently, he works as a painter as well as doing some construction work. Prior to becoming a member of the Christian Community, he explored Catholic retreats and Tibetan Buddhism.

Theresa Seufert, in her early thirties, joins us. Theresa is a Californian who, in college, majored in anthropology and minored in early childhood education. She is currently unemployed and is looking for a job as an apprentice carpenter.

"I felt that I had to get my act together," says Theresa about becoming a member of the Christian Community, "and so was drawn to the Community. I hope to build a relationship with our Lord Jesus Christ and serve Him in any way that I can."

The communion service is about to begin, and I go into the chapel. Reverend Bob Harrison comes out into the sanctuary and begins the service. Both the chapel and the communion service are reminiscent of the hundreds of Catholic churches and the thousands of masses I have attended during my lifetime. A major difference is that the approximately one hundred persons in the Christian Community chapel seem much more engaged in the liturgical service than I have seen during most Catholic masses.

After the service, the members of the Christian Community

mingle about and I have an opportunity to speak to the Reverend Harrison again.

"I'm quite impressed by the spirit of community here," I tell him.

"That's why this fellowship was started," he responds. "It's been my experience that many churches are only Sunday social occasions and others have only a liturgical service attended because of habit or requirement. We have lost the sense of the church, the 'ecclesia' as a group of persons both worshiping together and forming a community together. And that's what's happened here. This community is a living organism with Jesus as its strong central focus.

"As you know, this community doesn't meet to worship on Sundays: we gather every day—for the communion service, for prayers, for meditation. The network of community permeates our lives."

I leave the Christian Community of San Francisco. As I am walking out of the building, one of the women whom I had seen at the Holy Order of MANS' brotherhouse notices me. "God bless you, Mr. Fracchia," she says with a broad smile, "and please come back again."

8

The Charismatic Consciousness

Our Lady of Guadalupe Monastery

A RE you Charles? Hi, I'm David."
I was a bit startled as I looked up from my chair in the Santa Fe Municipal Airport. Can this man be the abbot, I thought to myself?

Dom David Geraets, the Benedictine abbot of Our Lady of Guadalupe Monastery in Pecos, New Mexico, was dressed in dark denim slacks with a loose white shirt over which hung a pendant, consisting of a cross with a white dove situated in the middle. His informal attire was accentuated by his crew-cut hair and a middle-aged paunchiness.

I recovered my composure sufficiently to mumble some words of greeting, and walked with him to a car in the parking lot for our drive to Pecos. On the way, I learned that the Abbot David, as he is called by the monastic community, was born and grew up in Wisconsin, and, after three years of college, joined the Benedictines at Benet Lake, Wisconsin. After finishing his course of studies there, and being ordained to the priesthood, he was sent to the Gregorian University in Rome, where he earned a doctorate in Missiology (a study that entails the social sciences, non-Christian religions, and other matters that might be related to the engrafting of Christianity on a given culture).

Upon his return to the United States in the late 1960s, Father Geraets taught at Benet Lake and at Dominican College in Racine, Wisconsin. During this time he became involved in the growing Catholic pentecostal movement. In 1969, his superior sent him to Benet Lake's foundation in Pecos, New Mexico, where he became prior in 1971 and abbot of the independent monastery a few years later.

We drive up to the monastery gates and into a complex of diverse buildings: a large adobe structure, wood-shingle cabins, log houses, and a building that resembles a factory. Father Geraets explains that the monastery property was originally a dude ranch and then a Trappist monastery before being acquired by the Benedictines, which accounts for the architectural hodgepodge. Numerous persons are wandering about the grounds, and Father Geraets explains that a week-long retreat for nuns is in progress.

I put my luggage in a room in one of the shingle cabins and wander over to the main building. A large chapel, a lecture hall, a cafeteria-size dining room, offices, and rooms for the monastic community are all contained in the building. There is a great deal of bustling about in every room: several persons are setting tables for dinner in the dining room, people are coming and going through the door leading to the offices, and small groups are gathering in conversation in the lecture hall and in an adjacent room.

"Are you looking for someone?"

I glance around and see a man who appears to be in his fifties.

"Oh, no, I'm just looking around," I respond. "Are you part of the community here?"

"I'm from Holy Trinity Monastery near Tucson: it's a foundation of Our Lady of Guadalupe."

We introduce ourselves and sit down at a table in a large room adjacent to the lecture hall. Cass La Veer tells me that he and his wife have made a three-year commitment to become part of the covenant community at Holy Trinity Monastery, and that they are visiting Pecos for a few days.

A covenant community, Cass explains to me, is a group of charismatics who wish to live together in order to pursue their spiritual life in a community and who make commitments to live in such a community for varying lengths of time.

"We have a Benedictine community," he says, "of about six persons and three married couples at Holy Trinity at the present time. But the community is open to single persons and married couples with or without children."

With obvious enthusiasm, Cass La Veer describes the community of Holy Trinity Monastery, its ninety-three acres, its schedule, the work done there, and the people who are part of the community.

"I was a traveling salesman for a jewelry concern," he says, "and, to be perfectly honest, battling alcoholism and arthritis. Around 1970, I began to become interested in the charismatic movement. My wife and I came to Pecos for a retreat, and I was healed here. In 1976, we decided to become part of the community at Holy Trinity Monastery. Our children were grown—so I just sold our house in Phoenix, retired, and went to Holy Trinity. It's been a joyful experience for my wife and me."

The charismatic covenant community as it exists at Our Lady of Guadalupe Monastery and at its foundation, Holy Trinity Monastery, is essentially a lay community (although members of religious orders are also menbers) alongside a community of Benedictine monks. An accepted applicant for a covenant community spends a trial period of at least four to six weeks in the community, conforming fully with its life, and participating in its prayer periods and work. At the end of the trial residence, the applicant is presented by the superior for a vote of the community that will grant acceptance for three months, six months, one year, or three years. At the end of the first three-year commitment, there is a possibility for another renewal, and it is hoped that this will lead to a permanent or lifetime commitment in the future.

During commitment periods other than final or lifetime commitment, members of Holy Trinity Monastery contribute at least 60 percent of their income to the community. If a member possesses little or no income but has financial assets, these assets may be contributed for the support of the member and his family. However, at the superior's discretion, those wtihout income or assets can also be admitted.

My conversation with Cass La Veer comes to an end when a bell rings, announcing dinner. We walk upstairs to the dining room, serve ourselves from a central table, and sit down at one of the tables. There are about a hundred persons at dinner—a combination of retreatants and members of the Pecos community.

Sitting at my right is a middle-aged man, casually dressed, who is addressed by a number of those at the table as "Michael." It turns out that he is Father Michael Sawyer, sub-prior of Our Lady of Guadalupe Monastery. A member of the original group of Benedictines sent from Benet Lake to found the monastery at Pecos, Father Sawyer was ordained a priest a few years ago.

"I've been a Benedictine monk for thirty years," he says, "and ordination to the priesthood wasn't something I expected. But my work increasingly has called for a sacerdotal ministry. I took some courses in theology, and the archbishop of Santa Fe ordained me."

I asked Father Sawyer about the confluence of a Benedictine monastic community with a lay community, and he responds: "I have never lived a more authentic Benedictine life than I have lived here: it springs from the spirit, not the law. I think this community represents the fullness of the Benedictine monastic tradition."

"What about the fact that there are women in the community?" I ask.

He smiles. "I think that having women in the community is one of the most valuable things about life here," he replies without hesitation. "The Pecos community, as you may know, is different from Holy Trinity, which takes married couples and children. Here the community is composed only of single men and women. We've all found that the importance of interaction between men and women in this community — and, mind you, we are all vowed to celibacy, even those who are in temporary commitment for the time of their commitment — is of inestimable value. The men and women in this community complement each other both in the process of day-to-day living as well as in our religious life. Being alive in the Spirit and being alive in our prayer life obviates the sexual aspect of men and women living together in a monastery. We are celibate and relate to each other as brother and sister, as part of being together."

Women in the Pecos community are excluded from becoming full members of the Benedictine community according to the present canon law of the Roman Catholic Church. Thus, although Geraets and Sawyer both emphasized that the community is looked upon as an integrated, single unit, the juridical reality is that it is divided into two parts: those who are Benedictines canonically (who can only be men at Pecos) and those who are part of the covenant community. At present, there are about twenty Benedictine monks (not all residing there) who form part of the Pecos community, and about thirty members of the covenant community.

"The women in the community are considered to be residential oblates under the Benedictine rule," Father Sawyer adds.

We linger over our coffee after dinner, and discuss this innovative monastic experience. "There is a great advantage to Our Lady of Guadalupe being in the Benedictine fold," Father Sawyer says. "We are part of a great monastic tradition, and our autonomy as a monastery allow us, under Church law, considerable room for experimentation. I feel privileged to live in a community of love."

It is almost 6:30 P.M.—time for Vespers—so we go to the chapel. The verses of the psalms sung for this portion of the divine music are alternated between one side of the chapel and the other.

At the conclusion of Vespers, the retreatants leave the chapel and go to the lecture hall. There, Sister Mary Jo McEnany, who has been a member of the Pecos community since 1972, but who is formally a nun of the Sisters of Charity of Leavenworth, Kansas, gives a talk to the retreatants. She wears no religious habit except for the distinguishing pendant—the cross with a white dove, signifying the Holy Spirit.

As with most of the women at Pecos, lay or religious, Sister Mary Jo McEnany conveys a sense of strong conviction and competence. After entering the Sisters of Charity in 1951, she taught grammar school, received her master's degree in special education, and worked with emotionally disturbed and retarded children in Santa Monica, California. It was there that she became involved in the charismatic movement. In 1971, she went to Pecos for a retreat, and the following year became a member of the covenant community. She is today in charge of arranging retreats at the monastery.

When she has completed her talk to the assembled nuns, we sit in the lecture hall and converse before going to the chapel for Compline. I ask her about her feelings concerning Pecos being a mixed community.

"Before coming to Pecos," she says, "I lived in a community of women for more than twenty years, and I must honestly say that I far prefer a mixed community. I know that skeptics or those who don't understand the Church's teachings on celibacy will laugh at this, but my own experience and that of people in the community here attest to the fact that you can have a celibate community composed of both men and women.

"Also, certain negative aspects of communities, either of all men or all women, are lessened in a mixed community. The women become less petty and the men become softer. The sensitivity of women to pain, loneliness, and unhappiness makes community life less harsh for men; and men are able to lessen the tendency of women to focus on the foibles of other women. Certainly, the women in this community have helped to bring out the gentleness in men."

We are called to Compline, which is being held in the lecture hall this evening, and we arrange to talk again later in the evening. Once more the psalms are chanted for this last of the day's Divine Office, after which we go into the chapel for a healing session.

The seating in the chapel has been changed. The chairs are arranged in small circles. The lighting is low, and a trio playing guitars are at one end of the chapel. The members of the Pecos community sit in chairs, of which one or two are left vacant in each circle for those who wish to seek to be healed.

The gift of healing, according to charismatics, can be applied to physical, emotional, and spiritual needs. Praying over the person, the laying on of hands, and the anointing with oil are all possible factors in this ceremony of healing.

Tentatively at first, some nuns sit in the vacant chairs. There is some murmured conversation—then the hands of the members of the Pecos community sitting in the circle reach out and are placed on them. The eyes of the members of the Pecos community sitting in the circle are fixed on the nuns or closed. Soon the room is filled with a babble of voices, sounding like the conversation at a large cocktail party—but the sounds are the prayers of those sitting on the chairs.

A tall, handsome, blonde woman enters the chapel. She is crying uncontrollably. One of the members of the community comes over to her and brings her to a vacant chair in one of the circles. I watch her talk tearfully to those sitting around her; and the hands of the group reach out to her. For ten minutes there is intense vocal praying: I can hear one of the groups continuously repeating the word *Jesus*. I learn the next day that the blonde woman and her husband came to Pecos for a retreat, and there had decided on a divorce.

What is this movement, so uncharacteristic of the Roman Catholic Church, that has sparked this moving and remarkable session of healing? Catholic pentecostalism—or as it is also called, the Catholic charismatic movement—can be traced to 1967, when some Catholic professors and students at Duquesne University in Pittsburgh experienced what the classical-pentecostals and neo-pentecostals (two Protestant-based pentecostal movements, which began at the turn of the century and during the 1950s, respectively) term the "baptism in the Holy Spirit." Within a few months, similar charismatic happenings took place at Notre Dame University, Michigan State, and other campuses. Soon, the charismatic movement was growing rapidly throughout U.S. Catholicism.

The Monastery of Our Lady of Guadalupe in Pecos, New Mexico.

A report of a meeting of U.S. Catholic bishops in 1969 stated that the movement does not ascribe to "the ideology or practices of any denomination, but likes to consider itself a renewal in the spirit of the first Pentecost." Admitting that the movement is soundly based, both biblically and theologically, the committee of bishops who prepared the report concluded that it should be given freedom to develop, under the pastoral supervision of the bishops and with the involvement of prudent priests.

As a result, the charismatic movement has become the fastest-growing and most vital aspect of Catholicism in the United States.

The charismatic movement propounds no new dogmas. Instead, it stresses the experiencing of the truths that Catholics already accept. If there is anything novel about the movement, it is the belief that the charisms, or gifts, of the Holy Spirit should play a larger role in the life of every Christian.

"Many people mistakenly equate pentecostalism with speaking in tongues," says Jim Scully, editor of Our Lady of Guadalupe's publishing venture, Dove Publications. "Without a doubt, Pentecostals have revived the charism of tongues, and it figures prominently in their literature. But we must avoid letting this cloud the picture. What we are really dealing with is a total view of Christianity seen in the perspective of the Holy Spirit. Pentecostals seek the fullness of life in the Spirit of Jesus. This embraces all the activities of the Spirit that we find in the Scriptures, including the spiritual gifts. One of these is tongues.

"Pentecostals are people of the Bible. They ponder God's Word to be well informed on God's plan and to take on the mind of Christ. In the New Testament they read frequently of the Spirit's connection with phenomena like tongues, prophecy, miracles, conversions, community, etc. So they are not surprised to see these same gifts and experiences happening to themselves and to all who will believe.

"And yet, charisms and religious experiences, wonderful though they be, must lead to higher things—the fruits of the Spirit. Love, joy, peace, patience, kindness, generosity, faith, mildness, and self-control give direction to the charisms and put them in proper perspective.

"So really, the important thing in the pentecostal movement is not the movement itself, but the Holy Spirit. The movement, whatever structure and organization it has or may develop, has value only insofar as it assists people to make Jesus Christ the Lord of their lives through the Holy Spirit."

The basic unit of the Catholic charismatic movement is the prayer meeting: and charismatics like to compare these to the close-knit communities of early Christians. In thousands of prayer groups around the country, weekly meetings offer the opportunity for spontaneous prayer, hymn-singing, and reading from the Bible. The sessions usually last several hours.

One of the charisms operative in these prayer meetings is the gift of healing. Jim Scully explains this gift: "Jesus cured people as a sign of God's love, power, and desire to save. He handed on this ministry to His disciples. Seeking to restore this dimension to ordinary Christian life, those in the charismatic renewal pray over the sick in the name of Jesus. Every prayer group can attest to the remarkable efficacy of this type of prayer."

The retreatants are no longer tentative in their seeking of the healing ministrations of the Pecos charismatics. They line up to take seats in the various circles as they become vacant. Earnestly and intently, they indicate to the group what they wish healed; and the charismatics in each group lay on their hands and pray out loud.

The number of those waiting to partake in the healing process dwindles, and the group in which Sister Mary Jo is sitting disbands. She comes over to where I am sitting, an we leave the chapel for the room adjacent to the lecture hall. There, we chat about the healing session that I had just witnessed, and about the healing ministry of the Pecos monastery.

"We believe that the Holy Spirit is calling us to utilize psychological methods for our healing ministry," she says. "A number of persons have influenced our work in this area: notably Morton Kelsey, who is a professor at Notre Dame, Ira Progoff, and Ruth Carter Stapleton. I suppose you could say that we are strongly influenced by Jungian psychology, as well.

"The utilization of dreams for the healing ministry is central to our work; and we recommend Dr. Progoff's journal system for keeping track of our dreams and interpreting them. Ruth Stapleton's active imagination work is another method we have used. Here, we isolate someone's fears that operate on his present life, and ask him or her to visualize each detail from the past that causes this problem. Then we encourage that person to imagine that Jesus is with him or her when that episode is taking place.

"For example, one man who was on retreat here could never hold a job for very long. Every time he was up for a promotion, he would panic and leave. We found that the reason for this was that he had gotten a sense that he was a failure from his parents, and that he would do anything to avoid failing. Well, we got him to visualize certain episodes from his childhood that gave him this sense of himself as a failure; and then we got him to imagine that Jesus was with him during this time. The healing results for this man were amazing."

This broad, Jungian-inspired healing ministry is a major factor in the spiritual ministry of Our Lady of Guadalupe Monastery. Morton Kelsey has come to give a retreat at Pecos centered around inner healing. Sister Mary Jo has taken the Progoff course on dream journal-keeping, and herself teaches its methods to retreat-ants. The writings of Ruth Carter Stapleton and John and Agnes Sandford provide insights and methods for the Pecos community's work in healing.

Physical ailments, as well as spiritual and emotional illnesses, are the objects for this work. "We are ourselves wounded healers," Sister Mary Jo tells me, "but the Holy Spirit works through us, imperfect though we are."

It is late when I return to the cabin where I am staying. From the porch I can see the Pecos River in the moonlight. For a short while I watch the lights in the rooms of the monastery buildings going out; and then I go inside and go to bed.

The chapel bell rings the next morning at 6:50 (an hour later than usual, because of the retreat). I shower, shave, and dress, and walk from the cabin to the chapel for Lauds. The chapel is filled with the members of the community and the nuns on retreat; and when the morning prayer has been chanted, everyone mills around waiting for the bell for breakfast to sound.

A friendly, attractive young lady sits next to me at breakfast. Her pendant identifies her as a member of the Pecos community. Heather Whitney is wearing a Radcliffe T-shirt, and, as we talk, she reveals to me that she is a graduate of that school. She is also an exception in a Catholic monastic community, for she is a convert to Catholicism.

In her late twenties, brought up in Delaware, with a degree in English literature from Radcliffe, Heather was raised in a Presbyterian family and educated in a Quaker grammar and high school. She describes herself as having been a religious child, and she tells me that she has been on a spiritual search since she was fourteen years of age.

"I became very much aware of the Spirit as a result of my having gone to a Quaker school," she says, "and for a period I was very attracted to Quakerism. But there are no visible sacraments in Quakerism, and I have always drawn great spiritual sustenance from the Lord's Supper."

After her graduation from Radcliffe, Heather went to George Washington University in St. Louis to study architecture. While on an excursion to St. Louis Priory to see its architecture, she met a monk who happened to be walking by. In the course of their conversation, he invited her to mass and a prayer meeting the following night.

"I went," Heather relates, "partly out of curiosity, I suppose, and was converted as a result. Out of that one experience Christianity made sense to me, and to that experience of the Eucharist I can date my conversion. If I had been a man, I would have entered St. Louis Priory on the spot."

But, not being a man, Heather Whitney could not. The prior at St. Louis Priory recommended that she go to Pecos; and in September, 1976, she became a member of the community.

"I would like to make a permanent commitment to the religious life," she continues, "and I plan to enter the oblate novitiate here whenever I can."

Heather's experience is unusual because very few persons not born Catholic are entering Catholic spiritual communities today. In fact, the reverse seems to be the case: many young Catholic men and women are flocking to Eastern and to Protestant evangelical and other non-Catholic Christian spiritual communities.

After breakfast, I wander over to a large modern structure that serves as the offices and warehouse for Dove Publications, the publishing venture of Our Lady of Guadalupe Monastery. Sister Eilish Ryan, a nun of the Sisters of Charity of the Incarnate Word, a member of the Pecos community, and the assistant editor of Dove Publications, gives me a tour of the building and describes to me the work of this specialized publishing venture.

"We put out about three books each year," she tells me, "and have about fourteen in print. In addition, we publish five pamphlets and about ten leaflets each year. We're not limited to material on the charismatic movement, but that's the bulk of what we publish. We also act as a distributor for spiritual and religious books and put out a newsletter that goes to almost 60,000 persons."

Sister Eilish takes great pleasure in showing me the solar heating system that was installed when the building was constructed. "It's 95 percent effective," she says proudly. "It's the only way to go, with the cost of propane and fuel. Once it's there, there's practically no overhead."

On the south face of the building there were 1,356 square feet of glass windows, serving as the solar collector, and 138 water-filled 55-gallon drums, used for heat storage. "I really feel that this is a help to the local people in the Pecos area," says Sister Eilish, "showing them how to build effectively. It's an educational thing—part of the Christian message. Ours is a simple lifestyle, and solar energy goes along with it."

The work aspect of the Benedictine motto "Work and Pray" is very much in evidence in the Dove Publications facility. Members of the community are bustling about, typing and performing a myriad of clerical tasks, working in the warehouse area, and filling orders for books. In addition, members of the Pecos community take turns cooking and setting up for meals, packing books for shipment, cleaning, sewing, bookkeeping, gardening, duplicating tapes, and assisting customers in the bookstore and giftshop. They also are involved in construction, maintenance, laundry work, and office and secretarial functions. A few of the community are directly involved in conducting the retreats that seem to go on constantly.

As I wander about the monastery grounds after leaving the Dove Publications facility, I find myself standing on the bank of the Pecos River by a teepee. I walk over to a member of the community who is digging in a nearby vegetable garden, and ask him about the teepee's use.

"Oh, that's where David Kreiter lives," he responds with a warm smile. "He's a new member of the community—interesting guy. Unfortunately, he's away for a few days. But you'd enjoy meeting him. He's the monastery clown—I mean that literally. He dresses up like a clown—white face, big red nose and all—and entertains the kids in the area. We're short of space here until those units you see being built over there are finished, but I think David lives there just because he wants to."

I walk up the slope of the hill towards the main monastery building. Groups of nuns are leaving the building after having attended a lecture given by Sister Mary Jo. One of them hails me and asks me what I am doing at Pecos. I tell her, and then ask her about her impressions of Our Lady of Guadalupe.

The kiss of peace punctuates mass at Our Lady of Guadalupe Monastery in Pecos, New Mexico.

"This has been one of the greatest weeks of my life," she says. "I'm sorry that it's coming to an end tomorrow. I've learned so many things here—and I've gotten such a basis for renewing my spiritual life."

The nun appears to be in her thirties. She is from a community in Arizona that teaches Indian children.

"Have you been involved in the charismatic movement before?" I ask.

"Oh, I've gone to a few prayer meetings, but that's about all," she responds. "But this experience has been so great for me that I'm going to become a member of a prayer group as soon as I get back to Arizona. The Holy Spirit has shown me the way."

She proceeds on to her room, and I continue walking to the main monastery building. A young man is locking up an alcove where the monastery maintains a small bookstore. His pendant identifies him as a member of the Pecos community, and I stop and chat.

Jim Steele is tall and handsome—in his late twenties. Born and raised in Chattanooga, Tennessee, he tells me that he is from a Catholic family, was educated in Catholic schools through high school, but fell away from the Church when he was a senior in high school and while he was at the University of Tennessee (from which he has a B.A. in English).

"I guess it was due to the changes which resulted from Vatican II," he says with a slight drawl. "Priests were leaving. There was a lot of confusion about what was right or wrong. The Church just didn't seem to have the same importance—or authority—as before."

Jim's return to the Catholic Church seems to have begun in the summer of 1971. He had been very much involved in drama at the University of Tennessee, and his theatre group had been performing plays in the inner city. At one such performance, a large group of young men descended on them, smashed their automobiles, ripped down the stage and scenery, and beat up the actors and actresses. Jim recalls that he kept repeating the name"Jesus" as he was being beaten. As a result of this carnage he was hospitalized.

"While I was in the hospital," Jim remembers, "my mother came to see me and asked that we pray together. She was in the charismatic movement, and I had seen what a profound effect it had had on her—not just spiritually, but on a lot of physical and emotional problems she had been having.

"When I got out of the hospital, I met a priest who invited me to attend a prayer meeting. I went to the meeting, and when I came back to my house I threw away my cigarettes and my drugs. I haven't smoked or taken drugs since.

"But something more had happened to me: I was very much taken with the feeling of community at the prayer meeting, and I began to get an indication that this closeness to God that I had witnessed was something that I wanted for my life."

After his experience of being beaten up while performing in the inner city, Jim had dropped out of college. Two years later, he enrolled again, and he received his degree in 1976. In July, 1977, he went to Pecos for a month's retreat, returning the following October for a three-month commitment.

"This community has been very important to me," he says. "We share each other's joys and sorrows. We help each other seek Jesus. I'm not certain where I'll be going: whether I plan to become a Benedictine or whether I'll eventually leave Pecos, start a career, and get married. But whatever I do, having been at Pecos for almost a year now has changed my life.

"One of the most significant aspects of life here is having a prayer partner. Because the community is very much of the opinion that the interaction between men and women is important to community life, each of us has a prayer partner of the opposite sex. During the day we get together and pray. And we also share each other's lives. When one is discouraged, or is sad about something, or has had some troubling experience, the other is there to share that experience and to help, if possible. You develop a real sense of caring for that person — a knowledge of the person's strengths and weaknesses. You want that person's happiness.

"I think this experience is invaluable for one in life. It's a wonderful preparation for pastoral work — and it's an excellent preparation for marriage."

Jim and I walk upstairs for lunch. The Abbot David pronounces grace, and each person sits down to eat. The conversation throughout the dining room is lively. The room is filled with the voices of nuns comparing their experiences during the retreat and of members of the community discussing logistics for coming retreats in the summer.

As I go to the serving table to get some dessert, I notice that one of the Benedictine priests of the community is sitting somewhat morosely at his table. A woman member of the community walks across the room and sits down in a vacant chair beside him.

"You look sad," she says. "Is everything okay?"

At first, he shrugs off her concern; but under her gentle prodding he reveals some disturbance.

"Why don't we take a walk and talk about it after lunch?" she says to him. And the priest agrees.

I notice that his moroseness has disappeared.

"Why don't we sit in my office and talk for a while when you're finished eating?"

I look up and see the Abbot David. A smile wreathes his face. One of the most sought-after retreat masters and spiritual directors in the United States, Abbot David Geraets is also one of the most human of men. I had noticed his interplay with the members of the community and retreatants: patient, warm, and playful.

Beneath his informality, however, one can see a capable and practical administrator, a core of inner strength, and a sense of
mission, fired by a vision.

We walk to his office, and he settles comfortably into an over-
stuffed chair.

"How are you enjoying your stay at Pecos?" he inquires.

I tell him that it has been a very interesting experience for me;
and I jokingly inquire if it's always as bustling as it has been during
my stay.

"Wait until our summer retreats begin," he says, "then you'll see
bustling. During the summer we have our family retreats, and the
place is filled with parents and their children—kids of all ages.
Members of the community take care of the younger children,
taking them on hikes and picnics—keeping them productively en-
tertained. It's a great experience."

"What other retreats do you give here?" I ask.

"We do introductions to Pentecost, pentecostal weekends on
key aspects of life in the Spirit, retreats for youth, Biblical
weekends, seminars for deacons and priests, five-day seminars on
spiritual growth, and thirty-day pentecostal experience programs.
Our apostolate is basically retreat work."

The abbot picks up a piece of paper from his desk. "Here's our
schedule for the rest of the year," he says, handing it to me. The
schedule lists a broad array of retreats and seminars: "Beatitudes
in Charismatic Renewal," "Charismatic Dimensions of Prayer,"
"Depth Psychology in Charismatic Renewal," "Covenant and
Community," and "New Life in Inner Healing" being just a few of
those listed.

"In addition we sent out teams of two or more throughout the
Southwest to give retrats, and we send out individual missionaries—
here in the United States, and to Mexico and Europe," he tells me.

"How does the community react to this activity?" I ask. "It
seems unusual for a monastery."

"Well, if you examine the history of Christianity, particularly
during the early centuries, you will see that Christians consisted of
small communities. The members of these communities not only
related to each other, but preached the 'good news.' I'm certain in
my own mind that what we call monastic communities originated
in a similar manner: communities of friends who wished to dupli-

cate the lives of these early Christian communities. They wished to help each other and to give witness to the world. And that's what Pecos is all about.

"The motive for people coming here is that they want to experience charismatic community living. True, Pecos seems radical in some ways for a monastery. Our use of psychology for our healing ministry, the fact that the community is composed of men and women, the large numbers coming here for retreats, are all unusual. But I think this is the 'new monasticism.' I think that our witness will eventually cause others to examine the roots of Christianity and to come up with some radical answers to questions."

Abbot David's secretary, Donna Ohmes, knocks on the door and tells him that he has an appointment waiting. I thank the abbot for his time, and walk out into the brilliant New Mexico sunshine.

At 3:45 P.M., a bell breaks my reverie. I pull out my copy of the Pecos schedule and notice that it is time for the Eucharist to be celebrated. I walk slowly from my cabin and take a seat towards the back of the chapel. A priest walks in and sits down in the front row of chairs. Another walks in and sits next to him. A third follows him and sits in a chair behind the altar—which is situated in the middle of the chapel.

Mass begins. The guitarists provide music. Hymns are sung. Readings from the Old and New Testament are given by members of the community. At the end of each reading there is a pause for meditation. When the gospel of the day is read, there is a moment of silence—then sounds begin to fill the chapel. At first there is an individual sound here and there—and then more and more individuals join in the chorus. The sounds resemble an orchestra tuning up.

One young woman, a member of the Pecos community, has her two arms uplifted. There is a look of rapture on her face. Slowly she repeats the word *Jesus . . . Jesus . . . Jesus.* A man sitting near her has his eyes closed. His arms reach high, and he is uttering words in a singsong that I don't understand. A rapid fire of words and phrases that sound like a made-up language come from yet another member of the community . . . and then he is silent.

The sound swells in the chapel . . . declines . . . and then all is silent. I look about me and see several faces rapt in silent prayer.

Father Stephen, the prior of Pecos, then makes a few comments about the Gospel just read. There is a moment of silence. Another member of the community gives a very personal account of the meaning of the text. Then one of the retreatants says a few words about the Gospel. Another period of silence is broken by the Abbot David, who comments on the reading. And then the celebration of the Eucharist resumes.

The "kiss of peace" takes several moments, as those in the chapel walk about, hugging each other, shaking hands, and joyfully offering each other "Christ's peace."

Two long lines then form for individuals to take communion, and shortly thereafter the mass ends.

The sense of a community worshiping together, so evident at the celebration of the Eucharist, continues at supper, which follows mass. There is a sense of joy, a sense of reaching out to one another, a sense, as one member of the community said to me, that "Jesus Christ is lord of past, present, and future."

I leave Pecos on a Sunday. The retreat for the nuns has ended. The community is off to Albuquerque to watch a performance of *Fiddler on the Roof*.

"I'm very excited about seeing it," the young man driving me to the airport tells me, "but what is most exciting is that the whole community shares this experience together."

9

The Search for Temporary Community
Pendle Hill and Vajradhatu

PENDLE HILL

Y OU mean you think Pendle Hill is a monastery?" laughed Jim
Best, who had just completed a year's residency and courses
at the Quaker institution. "That's interesting. Last year when I
told a friend of mine that I would be spending a year at Pendle Hill,
he said to me, 'Why are you going to that Quaker monastery?' "

Best's amusement that I would consider Pendle Hill a monastery
was not unjustified. (It is named, incidentally, for the hill in Lanca-
shire, England, where, in the seventeenth century, George Fox had
the vision that led to his founding the Society of Friends, or
Quakers, as they are commonly called.) With the exception of the
staff, which serves at Pendle Hill on a more or less permanent
basis, those who go to Pendle Hill do so for nine months only. No
vows are taken. The community's attractive setting in Wallingford, Pennsylvania, a suburb of Philadelphia, can hardly be considered a remote retreat from the world. Without the earmarks of
traditional monasticism, then, why consider Pendle Hill as part of
the "new monasticism"?

The clue to Pendle Hill's being considered in a study of the "new monasticism" in the United States is provided by the institution's brochures about itself: "a Quaker experiment in work, worship, and study," says one; "a Quaker center for study and contemplation," proclaims another. Pendle Hill's basis does not seem so different from that of some Benedictine monasteries I have visited. But what about the lack of vows? And the short-term commitment?

Is it not possible, I asked myself, that the essence of monasticism need not include taking formal vows? Is it not possible that the "new monasticism" could encompass a short-term commitment to "work, worship, and study" in a community environment designated for this purpose?

Founded in 1930, Pendle Hill slowly acquired property in Wallingford—near the colleges of Haverford, Swarthmore, and Bryn Mawr—and began its unique experiment. It remains today a tribute to Quaker vision and prudence.

My room at Pendle Hill was a charming garret in what is called the Main House—an old farmhouse in which the dining facilities, a large reading room, and rooms for sojourners (those staying at Pendle Hill as guests) are located. I had arrived late one evening, and the next morning arose at 7 A.M. for breakfast. This was a simple matter of cooking—or pouring—for yourself whatever you wished. Nevertheless, the quiet skill of the housekeeping staff was evident in the neatly arranged table laden with assorted cereals. juices, milk, eggs, and other breakfast foods.

By 8:30, I wandered over to a building known as The Barn—a congeries of offices, rooms for residents, a bookstore, and a meeting room. One of the features of Pendle Hill is the Quaker meeting for worship each morning. There were several persons already sitting quietly on pewlike benches when I arrived. For the first twenty minutes of the meeting, there was silence. One of the residents then stood up, made some comments, and then sat down. Silence again. After about ten minutes, a woman stood up and delivered some remarks about how grateful she was to the Spirit for leading her to Pendle Hill. There was another period of silence, and then somewhere off in the distance a bell rang. Those assembled in the meeting room stood up and began talking and greeting each other.

A very tall, handsome, youngish-looking man walked over to me, shook my hand, and announced, "Hi, Charles. I'm glad to meet you. I'm Parker Palmer." Palmer has the title of Dean of Studies at Pendle Hill, and although titles do not abound at the community, his office seems to be analogous to that of an executive director.

We walked over to the house where he and his family live — yet another charming Pennsylvania farmhouse — and discussed Pendle Hill. Palmer came here in the early 1970s, first as a resident, then as Dean of Studies, after a distinguished academic career that includes a B.A. from Carleton College, a Ph.D. in sociology from the University of California at Berkeley, and study at the Union Theological Seminary in New York. He spent five years as Senior Associate of the Washington Center of Metropolitan Studies before coming to Pendle Hill.

"My wife and I felt that we would like to live a life in community," he says. "We decided to spend a year at Pendle Hill. This position opened up while we were here, and we decided to stay on as staff members."

Palmer describes for me the basis for the Pendle Hill experience and the rhythms of life there. "We derive our inspiration, of course, from the testimonies of Quakerism: equality, simplicity, community, and harmony, I would say that the overall curriculum here is the life of the community.There is daily worship for the community, as you've seen. Beyond that period of worship, most of those here spend time in private meditation; and some engage in a variety of religious practices.

"Community life here at Pendle Hill means that everyone is involved. Our meals are eaten in common — staff, residents, and sojourners. The work of housekeeping, maintenance of the property, and anything else that has to be done for upkeep is performed by everyone. There is a rotation of daily tasks, and then there are designated work periods during the week to accomplish special tasks such as painting, mowing the lawns, and so forth. At the meeting for business, a session in which any problem connected with the community life may be considered, all residents, including sojourners, take part. Decisions are arrived at, according to the Quaker method, on the basis of unanimity without voting. There is no minority whose continuing dissent might give rise to friction between factions.

"Contemplation, worship, and study comprise the three basic components of the Pendle Hill experience. As to study, I would describe the basic educational fare as being courses for the inward journey and the outward reach, for the renewal of self and the building of community, courses for hand and mind and spirit."

I look at a description of courses for the three terms of the 1978—79 educational year. There are courses on crafts (weaving, pottery, and photography), one course entitled "The Journals of Thoreau: A Reading-Writing Workshop," and others called "Listening to Music," "Silence and Worship: A Study in Quaker Experience," "Records of the Life of Jesus," "William Blake: Creative Symbolist," "The Practice of the Presence of God: Personal Prayer and Corporate Worship," and "Contemplation and Action: A Study of Thomas Merton."

Mornings at Pendle Hill are devoted to study: the afternoons and early evenings are given over to classes.

This Quaker fusion of school and community has been described by a former director of Pendle Hill, Howard Brinton, in a booklet entitled *The Pendle Hill Idea*. He discusses how a community such as Pendle Hill falls between the family and the state in fulfilling man's needs for community. Pendle Hill makes "educational use of two basic Quaker principles: the importance of the small, integrated, religiously centered community as a starting point for a social order higher than that of the world in general, and the importance of immediate experience as a necessary supplement to beliefs and theories," he writes.

Counseling is provided for Pendle Hill residents, in that each student is assigned a staff advisor with whom he or she consults at least once a week. These consultations may concern personal problems or intellectual pursuits. However, Parker Palmer tells me, neither counselors nor teachers should be looked on as "gurus." "We provide, through communal learning in the context of the community, an option to the guru. Here, the *environment* is guru," he tells me.

About thirty persons come to Pendle Hill for each term. Fifteen or twenty of these stay for the entire year.

"What kind of people come to Pendle Hill?" I ask.

Parker Palmer laughs. "You could almost say that Pendle Hill is a 'halfway house,' " he says. "Most of the people who come here are at turning points in their lives. The ages range from seventeen to eighty. The average age is in the early forties. Some are married and come with spouses and children; some are single parents; and some are single. Usually, half the residents are Quakers; but Pendle Hill is an ecumenical community.

"You could divide those who come to Pendle Hill into three age-groups. There are those from seventeen to thirty or thirty-five. Many of these are dropouts from colleges or graduate schools, and are trying to arrive at decisions about their lives. The thirty-to-fifty age-group come here because of marital breakups, mid-career crises, or from a need for renewal. And the age-group of above fifty are usually recently retired or widowed.

A meeting for worship begins the day at Pendle Hill.

"These motivations for coming here, however, should be seen in spiritual terms. There are a number of places where people can go to resolve crises like divorce or to solve mid-career problems. But the environment at Pendle Hill seeks to free time and space. It offers a kind of hospitality. There is no burden of the expectations of others. And yet, there is discipline, the offering of challenges, and the importance of freedom."

We leave his house together and walk back to the Main House for lunch. The term has just ended at Pendle Hill, and the summer session has not yet begun. Today, only twenty or twenty-five persons are there for the meal. Palmer introduces me to one of the staff at Pendle Hill, an instructor by the name of Steve Stalonas, who is sitting at the table with us. An almost burly man in his late thirties, Stalonas is verbal and incisive. He came to Pendle Hill in

1972 to teach courses on social change; and his courses during the 1978–79 term include "Conflict and Cooperation," "The Witness of John Woolman," "Loaves and Fishes," and "Records of the Life of Jesus."

After lunch, Stalonas and I walk to his small, book-lined cottage. He tells me that he is from an upper-middle-class family, was born and raised in Manhattan, and attended the experimental New College at Hofstra University.

"In college and afterwards, I was active in social change," he tells me. "I worked for peace and was involved in the anti-war movement. I worked for prison reform, was a neighborhood organizer—the whole thing. Then, during the mid-1960s, I got into business. I made some money in an art business in New York, and then, with some friends, started a software computer company. We sold out for a lot of money to a large company. At the time I received my share of stock from the acquisition, I asked myself, 'What have I done?' My questioning was the result of several months of desperation, almost a 'dark night of the soul.' I felt that I had sold out, betrayed my principles. So, within forty-eight hours, I gave away all the money I had made to five different organizations whose principles of working for social change I endorsed. I started to feel clean again."

Stalonas has been a Quaker since 1969 and has devoted his life to the causes that have resulted from the testimonies of Quakerism.

I ask Stalonas why he feels that people come to Pendle Hill, and what they take away with them.

"Well, I think that people come here for different reasons; but when they're here, most of them become close and experience community," he responds. "Pendle Hill is a ministry of the Society of Friends, and within the Pendle Hill community the testimony of community takes place. The interdependence of the members expresses itself in many ways—spiritually, intellectually, economically, and socially."

Does he feel that he has changed as the result of his involvement with Pendle Hill?

"Oh, yes," he says with a smile. "I've learned to be more tender with people. I've learned not to gossip. Pendle Hill gives me a place to stand—a place where I don't have to make a lot of money—a place where I can be embraced when I'm at odds with the world—and it gives me a family."

There is a feeling of an Old Testament prophet about Steve Stalonas. His black beard and intensity, his occasional self-deprecating wit, appearing to cover a visionary's anger and impatience, and his outbursts of intensity all combine to rivet one to his thoughts and ideas. But the solitariness of the prophet is mitigated, in his case, by his sense of community.

"God calls me with a very loud voice," he says, as much to himself as to me, "and hammers on me. That hammering sometimes comes out in the form of the community."

I leave Steve Stalonas's cottage and walk back to the Palmers' home, a short distance away. Parker Palmer is sitting in the spacious living room, reading, when I am welcomed at the house by his wife Sally. Palmer and I plunge immediately into a discussion of Pendle Hill as "a place apart."

"Well, Pendle Hill is certainly a place apart," Palmer says thoughtfully, "The rhythm of our daily life, our expectations of self and others, the ways in which we meet, all differ from life's normal pattern. I do not mean that Pendle Hill is utopia or even that it is always better than what the world provides; in fact, there are days and weeks here when one would wish to re-enlist in 'real life.' I say only that it is different, and different with a purpose. Here is a place where 'life can be lived for its own sake,' where a person can pause, look around, go deep within, and emerge renewed."

The Pendle Hill Dean of Studies furrows his brow and looks out the window, pausing while he reflects.

"I began my stay here with misgivings," he continues, "and now and again they return. Many of my activist friends regard the inward quest as little more than an escape, a cop-out on responsibility to the world. Worse yet, I felt that impulse within myself: in coming to Pendle Hill, I had gladly walked out on several projects where I might — or should — have carried on. I am troubled by the possibility that the inward life is merely a way out of human obligation. If so, the indictment weighs heavily on me. For the God I know is the God of history, a God who works in the external world as well as within. For me, history is a place where we must respond to human suffering and human potential. We meet God in human affairs as well as in our hidden hearts, and if we only cultivate our soul's garden, our lives will not bear fruit."

And so the theme of "desert or city," of "escape or engagement," comes up again—this time at a Quaker spiritual and educational institution—and we talk about these issues until late in the afternoon.

Dinner on this warm, sunny evening is served on the lawn behind the Main House. I sit against a tree stump, balancing my tray on my lap.

"Do you mind if I join you?" asks an attractive woman in her thirties. "I'm Elaine Prevallet."

"Of course not," I reply. "Please sit down. Care for a tree stump?"

Elaine Prevallet, it turns out, is a Catholic nun who has been teaching at Pendle Hill for two years. Within a few days, she is returning to her order.

"Pendle Hill has been a very positive experience for me," she says. "It's been a nurturing community—we have ministered to each other—and I've found it a good balance between structure and freedom."

Born in St. Louis, Sister Elaine attended college in Denver before becoming a nun. She received a master's and a doctor's degree from Marquette University, and taught at Loreto Heights College for five years.

"I guess I beame tired of teaching young women who really didn't care about education," she says. "So I took a leave of absence for some studying and experiencing of my own. I have been, both personally and academically, interested in spirituality: so I spent time at the Integral Yoga Institute and at the Zen Center in San Francisco, and then went to Japan to spend six months in a Zen monastery.

"Parker Palmer invited me to come to Pendle Hill to teach, and I've taught courses on the New Testament, on Zen and Christianity, a course called 'Paths of Holiness,' and one called 'Prayer and Solitude.' "

When I ask Sister Elaine why she is returning to her order, she replies, "Oh, I just think it's time."

I have an appointment with a Pendle Hill student, Herta Joslin, who the next day will be returning "to the world." I bring my tray, dishes, and silverware into the kitchen, where a crew is already at work washing and drying, and walk to the reading room in the Main House.

I browse through some newspapers, periodicals, and journals,

waiting for Herta Joslin. The room has a high ceiling and resembles a reading room in a men's club—large, comfortable, and
quiet. A woman whom I had seen at meals and strolling around
the grounds walks in and introduces herself.

Herta Joslin wears her blonde hair in braids. She is in her forties,
married, and the mother of three children. She smoothes her long
peasant dress when she sits down opposite me on the long sofa.

"In a way, this has been like coming home for me," she says.
"My family lived here when I was young—they spent a number of
years on the staff. So I know Pendle Hill well. But this past year
has been like a sabbatical for me and my family. I guess you could
say that my husband and I came here to resolve our mid-life
crisis."

Herta Joslin went to New York as a young woman and became a
dancer, choreographer, and set designer. She married, had three
children, and moved to a small community in Connecticut. For
both her and her husband, the year at Pendle Hill was a time to
look at their marriage and to think about their careers. She is in
the process of shifting from her career in the theatre to one in psychology and therapy. The Joslins sold their house before leaving
for Pendle Hill, and now must determine where they wish to
live—as well as *how* they wish to live.

"I've always been a Quaker," she says, "but being at Pendle Hill
this year has given me a new spiritual dimension. I am more willing to let the Spirit work through me: I am much more willing to
let go. The spiritual aspects of community are very important in
Quakerism, and Pendle Hill is very much a spiritual community.
In all of its aspects, it has worked for me."

However, Herta Joslin affirms what Parker Palmer, Steve
Stalonas, and Elaine Prevallet had all said to me previously: that
the transitory nature of Pendle Hill—the nine months of intense
community, followed by dispersal—is frequently troublesome.
"But," says Herta, "this letting go is a spiritual discipline."

(Pendle Hill has a course each year called "Where Do I Go From
Here?" which seeks to implant in each Pendle Hill resident a sense
of new direction in his or her life after the Pendle Hill experience is
completed.)

After Herta leaves, I continue to browse in the reading room. I
come across a scrapbook that contains letters from former Pendle

Hill residents giving reflections and evaluations of their experiences at Pendle Hill.

"I like the way those in the second decade of their lives and those in the seventh are equally 'students,' and there is no 'faculty' but a 'staff' which includes more than teachers," writes a college professor from Michigan. "Staff are students who have remained; and the staff remain students in the deep sense: everyone is willing to learn from anyone. I don't worry too much about the 'unreality' of life here. Outer challenges are less harsh, to be sure, but there are profound inner ones. Busy-ness, too, can be an evasion."

"To be a student at Pendle Hill has been a challenge, a joy, a self-discipline, a nourishment: a challenge to live constructively with sixty others; a joy to know a wealth of caring, friendships, and unpressured pace; a discipline to find a right balance of personal space and community involvement; and a nourishment to be in a milieu where spiritual search and life have primary value," writes a woman who was in her mid-fifties when at Pendle Hill. "And because I have known the freedom here to simply be—time and support to follow spontaneous directions—I have learned better who I am by the choices I have made. What Pendle Hill does best, I think, is to support and encourage growing. This year is a unique and treasured experience—not always easy, many times fun, frequently stretching, and altogether valuable."

VAJRADHATU

It is said that the reason Chogyam Trungpa Rinpoche (the eleventh Trungpa Tulku, a direct incarnation of Karmapa, who was the founder of the karm-a-gyu school of Tibetan Buddhism) selected Boulder, Colorado, as his residence and as the seat of his spiritual empire is that it reminded him of his native Tibet—from which he was forced to flee by the Chinese Communists. I believed the comparison as I walked down Pearl Street, shivering in the January cold of this mountain community, looking for the offices of the Nalanda Foundation, one of the institutions set up by Trungpa Rinpoche for the dissemination of Tibetan Buddhism in the United States.

Joshua Zim, a staff member of the Nalanda Foundation, is awaiting me. We converse briefly, and he drives me to Marpa

House, a dormitory-style residence for the Karma Dzong community in Boulder. In this former fraternity house, about fifty men and women live, meditate, and also work at jobs in Boulder.

Jack Siddall, in his late twenties, the manager of the house, greets us and gives me a tour of the facilities. Siddall is from Las Vegas, Nevada, and received a degree is psychology from the University of Wisconsin. Following his graduation, he tells me, he was going to go to India because he felt the need for a spiritual teacher. However, he read about Trungpa Rinpoche in the *Whole Earth Catalogue*, and decided instead to come to Boulder. There he became a disciple of Trungpa Rinpoche.

About 55 persons live at Marpa House—two-thirds of whom are men. Some of the women live there with their children. Residents pay a modest monthly sum for food and rent. There is a small additional charge for classes.

As a community, Marpa House is a casual experience in comparison with many spiritual communities. Residents rise at 7:00 A.M., meditate in the house's large meditation hall from 7:30 to 8:30 A.M., have breakfast, and then go off to their jobs. Lunch is eaten at the places where they work (except on weekends). They return at 5:00 P.M., sit at meditation from 5:30 to 6:00 P.M., have dinner at 6:30 P.M., and attend class or engage in private study after dinner until 9:00 or 9:30 P.M. Free time for socializing is allowed after that hour.

Siddall tells me that only a handful of persons constitute the staff for Marpa House. "There is a manager and assistant manager, a chore master, a kitchen manager and an assistant kitchen master, a house fund-raiser, who is also a special events coordinator, and a maintenance person," he says. "All other residents work at outside jobs."

Karma Dzong, the Buddhist meditation and study center in Boulder, was founded in 1970, the year that Trungpa Rinpoche came to the United States from Great Britain. This center is the largest of the Vajradhatu centers in the United States. Most of its members live in private accommodations—in houses and apartments. Marpa House accommodates those in Boulder who wish to spend some time in a spiritual community. There are perhaps another twenty such communal houses in the United States.

"To be a follower of Trungpa's does not require one to live in a community," Joshua Zim tells me. "In fact, most do not. A place like Marpa House is for those who wish some reinforcement when they first become members of a Vajradhatu center. Most live here from one year to four years. It serves somewhat like a novitiate."

Marpa House allows residents to be introduced to Buddhist meditation and practice with others engaged in the same quest. An hour of daily meditation is required of each Vajradhatu member — whether or not he or she is a member of a residential center. The regime for residents of Marpa House is not entirely meditation and classes in various aspects of Buddhism, however. Poetry readings, speeches and lectures on a variety of subjects, picnics, live music, and even poker games are also featured.

Marpa House — a former University of Colorado fraternity house — now serves as a spiritual community for Vajradhatu Buddhism.

Jack Siddall is well-dressed. His mustache, curly hair, and handsome looks make one internally query if he might not be a holdover from Marpa House's fraternity house days. I ask him what kind of person comes to live at Marpa House.

"It's impossible to give a profile of the residents here," he responds. "In age, most are in their late twenties and thirties. They range from high-school graduates to holders of Ph.D.s. At present, we have lawyers, architects, nurses, dishwashers, and janitors. Boulder has a tough labor market, and a lot of our residents, who may be trained for more skilled jobs, will take lesser jobs. Most of the residents are single. Some come from wealthy families, others from poor families. We cover the entire range of socioeconomic backgrounds. And a large number of the residents come from strong religious backgrounds."

Each resident is required to take his or her turn at kitchen duties; and there is one workday a month in which all residents must take part.

In the kitchen at Marpa House, a small group of men and women are busy preparing the evening's dinner. I stop to talk to Greg Foley as he stirs the contents of a large pot. Foley's sandy-haired, blue-eyed, youthful appearance is not what one expects of a follower of Trungpa Rinpoche. He wears a school jacket with "Notre Dame University" emblazoned on its back.

"My father was a Notre Dame alumnus, and he wanted me to go there," Foley explains.

From Michigan, raised in a devout Catholic family, with a degree in sociology from Notre Dame, Foley arrived in Boulder—and began to live at Marpa House—in 1976.

"From my last couple of years in college, I became interested in the spiritual life," he says to me, still hovering over the pot. "I didn't find what I wanted in Catholicism, which, because of my background, became the first religious group considered. My interest in Vajradhatu came as the result of my coming to Boulder for a vacation after graduation. I went to hear Trungpa talk, and thought that he really made sense. I decided to stay in Boulder to learn more about Buddhism, became a member of Karma Dzong, and decided to live at Marpa House."

Foley goes on to tell me that his spiritual yearnings began as the result of his believing that there was something more in life than what he saw his classmates wanted, or what he saw was being achieved by his parents and their friends.

"I was no saint at Notre Dame," he says, "but it didn't take much for me to realize that drinking beer, 'getting laid,' hoping to get a job as an industrial salesman or to go on to law school, getting married, and having children weren't the end results of life. Also, I saw the results of all these strivings in my parents' friends and in the parents of my friends at college: all they can talk about is golf and football, they are overworked and bored, their marriages are empty, they have no relationships with their kids. I couldn't see it."

The Vajradhatu Buddhist experience calls its followers to participate in meditation practice, study, and work. These activities
are known as the three wheels of the dharma, and they are intrin-
sic to Karma Dzong. According to Buddhist thought—and the
teaching of Trungpa Rinpoche—the three wheels complement
each other: sitting meditation stimulates intuitive insight into our
own nature and that of all phenomena; study sharpens the
intellect and makes intuition more precise; work provides a solid
ground for application of intellect and intuition in daily life,
enabling us to take full responsibility for the practicalities of
living in the world.

Each meditator at Karma Dzong, and at Vajradhatu meditation
centers throughout the country, receives ongoing instruction in
the practice from one of Trungpa Rinpoche's authorized meditation
instructors. Buddhist meditation is a technique of resting the mind
in its natural state, neither holding it back nor allowing it to
wander.

Study is of Buddhist scriptures and commentaries, which can
correct and further inspire the practice of meditation.

Work connects the student to the ordinariness of the world,
Trungpa teaches. "Right livelihood" has been a prominent theme
throughout the history of buddhadharma. Right livelihood means
not only working hard for a living, but also bringing the precision
of meditative experience and intellectual understanding into one's
daily life. Most Karma Dzong members work at regular jobs. They
take full part in the normal pattern of U.S. life, raising families,
running businesses, buying homes, and relating with their neighbors. There is no attempt to remove oneself from the world.

Zim, Siddall, and I look into the large meditation hall at Marpa
House. Several persons are sitting on black cushions in the hall,
facing an elaborate shrine to Buddha. One of the women meditating leaves as I complete my inspection of the hall, and I am
introduced to Courtney Hale, who is in her late twenties and lives
with her two-year-old daughter at Marpa House.

"This has been the greatest, most transforming experience of my
life," says Courtney, referring to her coming to Boulder, becoming
a disciple of Trungpa Rinpoche's, and living at Marpa House.
Courtney Hale grew up in Connecticut in an upper-middle-class
household, attended an Ivy League college, married an ambitious

recent graduate of Harvard Law School, had a child, and lived in Manhattan.

"Life began to fall apart shortly after Jennifer was born," Courtney continues. "Jim, my husband, was intent on becoming a partner in his law firm and making a lot of money. I began to have second thoughts about the life I had chosen for myself; and when Jim and I separated and divorced, I was shattered. I wondered who I was, what was going to happen to me.

"My parents gave me a ski holiday to Colorado, and while I was in Boulder, some people told me about Trungpa. I went to one of his lectures, was turned off by the scene, but kept thinking about things he had said. Pretty soon I became more and more intrigued with what he was talking about, and went to hear him again. He was probably the most sane man I had ever encountered. Well, I started to meditate and started to go to classes on Buddhism. I went back to Connecticut, got Jennifer, and moved to Marpa House. I was tired of not having control of my life, I decided. I was going to take hold."

Courtney Hale goes on to say that she works as a waitress in a Boulder restaurant during the day, and that this life allows her sufficient time for her child and for meditation and studying Buddhism.

"I feel that not only is my life becoming sane," she says, "but that I am giving Jennifer a sane life. There is a lot of love for her and for me here; and the opportunity to assimilate Trungpa's teachings will set us both on the right path."

Joshua Zim drives me to the national headquarters for Trungpa Rinpoche's spiritual complex later that day. With the exception of the Naropa Institute, Trungpa's successful Buddhist university and educational center in Boulder, the other spiritual activities of Trungpa Rinpoche are run from this building in downtown Boulder. We walk by several secretaries and through a businesslike operation that resembles the executive suite of a successful entrepreneurial corporation more than the center of a spiritual movement.

We walk into a large office where Eric Weiss and Carl Springer are waiting for us. Weiss grew up in Los Angeles, met Rinpoche, and went to New York to study with him. He then received his degree in philosophy from the University of California at Santa

Cruz and joined the Nalanda Foundation staff in Boulder. Carl Springer, looking elegant in a three-piece suit, grew up in Manhattan and graduated from Brandeis University in sociology in 1971. He met Rinpoche through some classmates who brought him to hear one of Rinpoche's lectures, and was impressed by him. After graduation, Springer went to live at Karme-Choling, Trungpa's meditation center in Vermont, became the director of the Naropa Institute in 1975, and now has the title of director of external affairs for Trungpa's operations.

This network center is primarily concerned with keeping in communication with the more than fifty Vajradhatu meditation centers in the United States. These range from such large facilities as Maitri Center in Connecticut, Karme-Choling, the Rocky Mountain Dharma Center in Colorado, and Karma Dzong to meditation and study centers in San Francisco, Berkeley, and San Antonio, Texas. Of these latter centers, some are residential, others are not.

Members of the Vajradhatu centers are required to meditate twenty-seven hours a month under the guidance of a meditation instructor and to make the payment of dues. Those who do not conform to these requirements are suspended from the community.

"Living together in a community is not part of our practice," says Weiss, "but a number of persons do live in our meditation centers around the country because they feel that this is important for them for some reason or other — perhaps because community life provides reinforcement for them during their early years of meditating and studying."

"Some persons might think that we're very 'laissez-faire,' " says Springer. "We have no ban on smoking, drinking, or any sexual practices. There is a whole range of commitment and practice that is possible in the Vajradhatu, however. For example, we have long periods of meditation at Karma Dzong. The Rocky Mountain Dharma Center, about eighty miles north of here, provides the facilities and contemplative setting for group and solitary meditation retreats, intensive training sessions, workshops, and study programs. Karme-Choling is even more intensive.

"Adaptation is the key. Traditionally, Buddhism has traveled widely from where it began and has adapted to each culture in which it has become established. Sometimes people confuse the spiritual teaching and the cultural manifestations in which these teachings were historically set. So we have to ask ourselves whether the dietary, clothing, and ritualistic practices of 2,500 years ago in India are essential to Buddhism in the United States during the 1970s. I think we have to look at the road and not at the scenery."

The fact that tens of thousands throughout the United States have chosen to follow the Vajradhatu path is a tribute to the adaptation policies of Trungpa Rinpoche and his organization. But adaptation has also been the keynote of most traditional Christian churches and Jewish congregations in the West, and many of the thousands who meditate each day at Vajradhatu centers have come from these churches and synagogues. It has to be more than adaptation.

Perhaps the clue is provided by the words of Trungpa Rinpoche in *The Myth of Freedom and the Way of Meditation*:

> In Buddhism, we express our willingness to be realistic through the practice of meditation. Meditation is not a matter of trying to achieve ecstasy, spiritual bliss or tranquility, nor is it attempting to become a better person. It is simply the creation of a space in which we are able to expose and undo our neurotic games, our self-deceptions, our hidden fears and hopes. We provide space through the simple discipline of doing nothing. Doing nothing is very difficult. We must begin by approximating doing nothing and gradually our practice will develop. So meditation is a way of churning out the neuroses of mind and using them as part of our practice. As with manure, we do not throw our neuroses away but we spread them on our garden; they become part of our richness.[1]

1. Trungpa Rinpoche, *The Myth of Freedom and the Way of Meditation* (Berkeley, Calif.: Shambala, 1976), p. 2.

10

A Return to
the Rule of St. Benedict

The Monastery of Christ in the Desert

W HAT was I doing here, I asked myself? It was a hot Friday morning in the high desert country of New Mexico, and I was hoeing the dry clods that would form the vegetable garden for the Monastery of Christ in the Desert. My back ached from this unaccustomed labor, and I was wet and uncomfortable. I was also hungry. I had arrived the day before, driving about a hundred and fifty miles from Albuquerque—the last fifteen miles along a tortuous, rutted road that perched perilously above the deep-running Chama River. The monks at Christ in the Desert had already eaten their daily meal by the time I arrived. I had not eaten all day, and the next meal was not scheduled until today at 3 P.M. By the time I sat down to eat in a few hours, it would be just about two days since I had had any food.

A bell ended my "woe is me" reverie. Placing my hoe on the ground, I trudged across the field towards the chapel for Tierce—one of the canonical hours of the Divine Office. The ochre-colored adobe chapel nestled at the foot of the 500-foot-high Mesa de los Viejos, blending into the reddish soil and rocks that compose most of this Rio Arruba country.

I stopped for a moment to gaze at the mountains, which are part of the rugged San Juan range. They give the area a feeling of soul-swelling beauty. The austerity of the landscape is softened by a fair amount of vegetation: tall grass and cottonwood trees along the river, and bushes and trees in the crevices of the canyon walls.

I entered the church through the carved double wooden doors. A magnificent simplicity characterizes the structure. Designed by George Nakashima, it is typical of the Spanish colonial architecture of New Mexico, yet appears contemporary. The thick adobe walls of the Greek cross-shaped structure support a two-story, eight-sided nave. A slender bell tower rises from one corner of the exterior of the church, two arms of the cross forming two chapels: one for the Blessed Sacrament, and the other containing an unusual statue of the Virgin Mary. Peeled cottonwood sticks supported by giant Ponderosa beams form the ceiling. A few wooden benches provide seating accommodation. The altar—a slab of fieldstone supported by a stone pedestal—sits in the middle of the church. The eastern side of the building is a solid glass wall, affording a magnificent vista of the red cliffs of the Mesa de los Viejos.

Three young monks emerge from the sacristy. Bowing toward the tabernacle, they take their places in the choir stalls, which are built of weathered wood from a barn. One of them takes up a guitar, another a recorder. The prior, Brother Philip, begins the chanting of Tierce. The response is chanted by Brother Michael and Brother Jeremy. Back and forth goes the chanting of the psalms, alternating between those sitting on one side of the church and those on the other side.

In about twenty minutes, Tierce is finished. I leave the church and wander about the monastery grounds. Next to the church is the "convento"—a low-lying adobe building with a greenhouse along one side that houses the monastery's library, the refectory or dining room, the kitchen, and an office. A hundred yards further on, situated along the two sides of a dirt lane, are the cells of the monks: small adobe buildings that each contain two cells—small rooms, simply furnished with a bed, desk and chair, and some bookshelves. Beyond the cells are three or four buildings that serve as the workshops for the monastery. One structure, which had been the farmhouse for the ranch that was situated on the property before it was purchased for the monastery, now houses a gift-

shop. And about a half-mile down a dirt road is the guest house —
two wings of adobe buildings that contain nine rooms for guests.

I sit in the courtyard of the guest house. A bird perches on the
shoulder of a life-size wooden statue of St. Francis of Assisi
created by Santa Fe santero Ben Ortega. It watches me read, then
flies away when the church bell peals, announcing that Sext — another
of the hours of the Divine Office — is going to be chanted.

At the conclusion of Sext, shortly after noon, I walk with
Brother Jeremy to the "convento." We sit in the cool library.
Brother Jeremy is wearing blue jeans and a loose blue cotton
denim hooded shirt with a black belt. This is the habit of the
monks at Christ in the Desert — comfortable and practical for
these young men who alternate between their work and the singing of the Divine Office. In cold weather, a brown woven poncho is
also worn.

Brother Jeremy is in his late twenties. Born in Michigan, he
graduated from the University of Michigan with a degree in
anthropology. During his sophomore year, he became involved
with a Catholic charismatic community, and after graduation he
served as the administrator for the charismatic group. His desire
for a communally oriented religious life led him in 1976 to enter a
Trappist monastery in Iowa — which, after a year, he left.

"I had a desire to become a priest when I was in grammar
school," says the young monk, "but in high school and college I
had a girlfriend and put the idea aside. After college, however, I
became more and more attracted to a contemplative monastic life,
and decided to join the Trappists. But what developed was that I
got a clearer idea of what I wanted in monastic life: a smaller community and a community in which the members would support
each other in living their vocations."

The Trappists told Brother Jeremy that Christ in the Desert
would probably fulfill what he desired in a monastic community,
and, after a visit, he joined the monastery in late 1977.

Brother Jeremy looks at his watch. "I've got to ring the bell for
None," he announces. We walk to the church through an enclosed
garden. Brother Jeremy pulls the rope that dangles above his rustic
choir stall, and the bell in the tower responds with melodious
peals, summoning monks and guests to this portion of the day's
Divine Office.

None is a jubilant experience for me: the day's meal is to follow. At 3 P.M., the monks and the several guests file through the refectory into the large kitchen, and there they fill their plates with the simple but ample fare. I cut two large slices of bread baked by the monks, take a heaping helping of salad, and an enormous portion of beans. Then I stand at my chair, waiting for the last person to take his place. Brother Philip says grace and reads the day's martyrology and passages from a recent biography of Bishop Lamy, the nineteenth-century French missionary bishop of Santa Fe (and the subject of Willa Cather's *Death Comes to the Archbishop*), while all others eat in silence.

A Benedictine monk at Christ in the Desert Monastery in New Mexico plants flowers near the guest house.

Brother Jeremy brings the serving plates to each table for those who wish more food. I help myself to yet another portion from each plate. When everyone has eaten his fill, Brother Philip ceases to read and says grace.

The guests help the monks wash the dishes, and then they wander into the giftshop, where Brother Jeremy will assign work tasks to everyone. Some of the guests go to the fields to work. The monks at Christ in the Desert have been attempting to become more self-sufficient in providing their own food. Consequently, a large vegetable garden is being cultivated. Brother Philip had been working on a tractor that morning, renovating long unused irrigation ditches. This afternoon, Brother Michael and a few of the guests will prepare the ground for some additional planting. A 600-square-foot greenhouse adjacent to the "convento" was constructed with the help of the New Mexican Solar Energy Association for the dual purpose of growing food and providing heat during the winter months.

Other guests, including myself, go to one of the workshops with Brother Jeremy to help with weaving, which is one of the ways the community helps to support itself. The weaving of ponchos, liturgical vestments, rugs, and wall hangings has long been a major source of revenue for the Monastery of Christ in the Desert. No skilled work is required of us, however: we simply help to put some wool on the looms.

It is almost 6 P.M. when the workday is finished. We leave the workshop and see in the distance those guests who had been laboring in the fields walking towards the guest house. There, we all wash and then hurry to the church when we hear the bells calling us to the chanting of Vespers and Compline.

The monks have taken their places in their choir stalls. The handful of guests sit on the benches. Brother Philip once more intones "O, Lord, come to our assistance," and Vespers, evening song, begins. Whenever the doxology "Glory be to the Father . . ." is chanted, all make a profound bow. At the conclusion of Vespers, Brother Michael reads a selection from the works of John Cassian, an early writer on Christian spirituality. The section read deals with how monks should lead their lives.

Compline begins at about 7 P.M. When the last psalm has been sung, the monks and guests gather in the chapel of the Blessed Virgin Mary, sing a hymn, and then are blessed by the prior in a traditional ceremony whereby the head of the monastery blesses his "children" at the end of the day. Each of us bows as Brother Philip sprinkles us with holy water.

The sun has gone down by the time we leave the church, but it is still light and the air is warm. A stillness broken only by the occasional chatter of birds pervades Burns Canyon. The Chama River glistens as I walk back to the guest house.

I sit reading in front of my door, looking up frequently to watch the change of colors on the walls of the mesas as it grows darker. Finally, I go inside my room and light the kerosene lamp.

It seems as if I have been asleep for only a short while when the jangling of my alarm clock awakens me. It is 3:45 A.M., according to my watch, which I look at after I have fumbled with some matches—time for morning vigils.

I dress, grab a flashlight, and walk along the road that leads from the guest house to the church. A few other guests also enter the church, take their places on benches, and await the arrival of the three monks.

At 4 A.M., the monks enter, sit at their choir stalls, and proceed to chant the prayers of this beginning of the day's Divine Office. Not even the beauty of the psalms and other prayers can ward off the tendency towards drowsiness that afflicts me during the next hour and a half. Through the glass wall of the church I can see the first light of dawn; and although the sun will not clear the mountains for some hours, the church begins to fill with light.

After vigils, I return to my room and sleep for another hour before I once more hurry to the church at 6:30 A.M. to participate in the singing of Lauds, followed by the Eucharist. I pull my sweater more closely around me, for it is cold. Brother Philip, in a colorful poncho, stands at the altar. Brother Michael, Brother Jeremy, and the guests stand around the prior. We eat the morsels of bread that Brother Philip gives us at Communion, and then take a sip of wine from the large stoneware cup that serves as a chalice. "The mass is ended, go in peace." We file out of the church and wait patiently by the "convento" gate until the sounding of the bell tells us that we may go into the refectory for breakfast.

I pour some cornflakes into a bowl and cover them with milk. The refectory is bereft of monks—since they eat but one meal a day—and the guests eat in silence.

After breakfast, I read in the library. I come across a passage from that superb commentator on monastic life, Thomas Merton, about Christ in the Desert:

> In America, there is no new monastic foundation which has found so perfect a desert setting as that of the Chama Canyon, in New Mexico, where the small Benedictine Monastery of Christ in the Desert now stands.
>
> . . . .
>
> The Monastery of Christ in the Desert is only in its beginnings: it is a small seed, seeking to fix its roots firmly in the rock and sand of the canyon, like the hardy piñon pines around it. It does not have the

monastic ambitions of the big institutions which have become famous, for one reason or other, in various parts of the country. It seeks only to keep alive the complete simplicity of authentic Benedictine monasticism in its most primitive form: a communal life of prayer, study, work and praise in the silence of the desert where the word of God has always been best heard and most faithfully understood.

As Merton found it during his visit in 1968 (when he was traveling towards his fateful destination of India for a conference of monks from the West and the East), so Christ in the Desert is today.

Founded in 1964 as a foundation of Mount Saviour Monastery in Elmira, New York, Christ in the Desert has not had an easy decade and a half of existence. Its founder, Father Aelred Wall, left the monastery to become a hermit in Mexico. Monks came and went. The current five monks who comprise the community (two were away during my visit) represent a hoped-for stability for the monastery. A renewal of purpose and a settling down after the "shake-out" of the post-conciliar period give indication that Christ in the Desert will now fulfill its promise of "keeping alive the complete simplicity of authentic Benedictine monasticism in its most primitive form."

Brother Michael Henderson, a strand of his reddish hair falling over one eye, walks into the library and sits down in a chair across from me. There is little trace in the speech of this former-Jesuit-turned-Benedictine-monk of his upbringing in Louisiana. Raised in a Catholic environment, desiring early in life to become a priest, and attracted to the Jesuits (with whom he spent six years) because of their academic orientation, Brother Michael found himself desiring more time for formal prayer than the Jesuit way of life allowed. However, the life of scholarship also attracted him; and he spent time pursuing Biblical studies in Cambridge, Massachusetts, and at Claremont College in California (where he helped translate and edit the Nag-Hamadi texts).

A visit to Christ in the Desert during the summer of 1974 confirmed Brother Michael in his growing desire for a monastic life; and in early 1975 he became a member of Christ in the Desert.

"I'm going to be spending some time each year studying," says Brother Michael, "but I made a conscious decision to give up a life of scholarship. Christ in the Desert, unlike most Benedictine monasteries in the United States which undertake a teaching apostolate, has no active apostolate. We do follow the injunction of St. Benedict that all guests should be received as Christ, and our guest house is always filled with men and women, Catholics and non-Catholics, who wish to spend some time here. We don't give directed retreats; we're more concerned with integrating our guests in our life of work and prayer.

"I would say that Christ in the Desert is characterized by a return to interpreting the *Rule* of St. Benedict literally, to return to the life lived by the early monks. Thus, we pray a longer Divine Office than is usual today in monasteries, eat only one meal a day, following the suggestions of the *Rule* as to when it should be eaten, and open up possibilities to members of the community for solitude. But our emphasis is on community life, the relationships of the monks one to another, and an emphasis on the superior — our prior, Brother Philip — being our spiritual father rather than the chief administrator. The *Rule* says that the abbot takes the place of Christ in the community. And we're into living a self-sufficient lifestyle — one in which our work provides us with our simple needs."

This search for an authentic Benedictine spirit — or perhaps more accurately, a return to the monastic life envisaged by St. Benedict — is very much a hallmark of contemporary Catholic monasticism. Whether it is felt that the needs of American Catholicism in the nineteenth century and during the first half of the twentieth century are no longer operative to justify an active apostolate among the traditional monastic orders, or whether our contemporary culture seems much more imbued with a spirit of contemplation and solitude, the fact is that the interest in Catholic religious life today seems centered in the more contemplative orders.

Paradoxically, as an increasing number of monastic foundations, like Christ in the Desert, seek a life more attuned to that of St. Benedict's *Rule*, their attraction becomes greater. Priests, nuns, and the Catholic laity have flocked in growing numbers to monasteries for spiritual invigoration. Their experience in these communities has not been that of a traditional retreat complete with conferences given by a retreat director, but a participation in the ordinary life of prayer and work led by the monks.

The desire for a more intense spirituality seems not to be met in the parish life of U.S. Catholicism. The barren nature of parochial Catholicism was highlighted by conversations with a number of Catholic laypersons whom I encountered at the monasteries I visited. "I have been interested in a more intensive prayer life," one recent convert to Catholicism told me, "but when I discussed this with my pastor, he told me that it was a sufficient if I went to mass every day." "Have you ever seen a notice in a parish bulletin," one man asked me, "that announced a class in the parish on techniques for meditation?" Even more damning was a woman's account of the derision she met with from her parish priest when she suggested that Lauds be chanted in the parish church before morning mass and that Vespers be chanted in the early evening. One man asked his parish priest for help in learning how to recite the Divine Office each day. "Do you know what he said?" the man indignantly inquired of me. "He said, 'It's a pain in the ass for us priests to say it. Why do you want to do it?'"

The lack of response of the diocesan clergy to the growing desire of the Catholic laity for more meaningful community life, a more fulfilling sense of liturgical worship within the context of such Christian community, and a more intense life of prayer tempts one to remark upon historical parallels: namely, those that indicate Catholic religious renewal coming basically from monastic energy — the spread of both Celtic and Benedictine monasticism during the early Middle Ages, the reforms of the tenth and eleventh centuries, the mendicants of the twelfth century, and the monastic revival in such orders as the Society of Jesus during the sixteenth century. Will a renewal in post-conciliar Catholicism, one asks, come from a renewal in monasticism? Will future vitality in U.S. Catholicism develop outside of parish structure?

There is a sense of the prophetic Church about such men as Brother Michael; they convey a feeling of excitement about their relationship with God; and the witness of their lives transcends the beauty of their physical surroundings. To the Catholic laity — who are used to unimaginative administrators of the physical plant of a parish, who see the clergy only at the celebration of mass and at an occasional sacramental function, and who observe their pastors as promoters of bingo games and bazaars — the parish priest seems remote from their increasing concerns to live a life closer to God and, possibly, within a meaningful community. It is for this reason that monasteries now have waiting lists of those wishing to spend time there.

The church bell rings, telling us that it is time for Tierce. The regular rhythms of the day continue—Sext, None, the meal in the refectory, work, Vespers, Compline, time for reading and for thinking. That evening I go to bed early, for Sunday mornings (and the mornings of holy days) represent somewhat of a departure from the usual schedule. Vigils begin at 1:15 A.M. and last until 6:30 A.M.

This Sunday morning, therefore, my alarm clock rings at 1 A.M. Once more, I find my way in the blackness of the night to the monastery church.

"O, Lord, come to my assistance," intones Brother Philip, and the marathon chanting of the Divine Office has begun. The chant is as follows:

> I lift up my eyes to the mountains:
> where is my help to come from?

Brother Philip and those guests sitting on his side of the church, accompanied by Brother Jeremy on the guitar, begin to chant Psalm 121:

> Help comes to me from Yahweh,
> who made heaven and earth.

Brother Jeremy and Brother Michael, along with the handful of guests on the other side of the church, chant the next verse.

> No letting our footsteps slip!
> This guard of yours, he does not doze!,

Brother Philip continues.

> The guardian of Israel
> does not doze or sleep,

respond Brother Michael and Brother Jeremy and myself.

The psalm's injunction does not seem to work. After an hour or so I am in agony. My chin drops to my chest, and I only vaguely hear the chanting in the background. My back aches from having to sit up straight on the bench. Brother Jeremy had warned me earlier that I would be both sleepy and stiff, and had encouraged me to walk around and to make myself comfortable in any way I could. I step outside and breathe some chill, bracing air, come back into the church, and this time sit on a bench against the wall.

The chanting of the psalms is alternated with readings from Scripture and from spiritual writers. A solemnity accompanies the beginning of such readings: whichever monk is reading takes the book, walks across the church to Brother Philip (or, when Brother Philip reads, to Brother Michael or Brother Jeremy), kneels before him and asks his blessing, and is blessed by the prior before going to the lectern to read.

An adobe gate leads into the Monastery of Christ in the Desert.

I find that despite my periodic drowsiness I am able to concentrate on the readings and on the chanted psalms. A more meditative comprehension of the psalms seems to be the result of the stately chanting of these intimate poems. (The chant is a sprung rhythm utilized by the Jesuit Gelineau in setting the psalms to music.)

The hours go by. Traces of light appear, glimmering through the glass window of the church. It is almost 6:30 when Vigils are over. Flecks of red stand out in the eastern sky as I walk to the guest house. A profound feeling of peace has grasped me, mirroring the quiet of this New Mexican landscape.

After breakfast, I sit with Brother Philip in the library. This jovial monk in his mid-tirties came to Christ in the Desert in 1974, after having been a monk at Mt. Angel Abbey in Oregon for ten years. He became prior of Christ in the Desert in 1976, and in the following year was ordained a priest.

"I wanted to be involved in a more radical form of monasticism," he tells me. "That's why I came to Christ in the Desert. I taught at Mt. Angel, but felt that I wanted to get back to a nonactive apostolate—which is what has been traditionally the hallmark of monasticism—a centering on being present in the Lord."

Brother Philip goes on to explain that the importance of community is also a factor at Christ in the Desert. "Many monastic communities have gotten quite large," he says, "which, along with an active apostolate, does not allow the monks to form supportive relationships with each other. We don't want to grow larger than a community of twelve or fifteen here; and each of us sees the community as a family."

The conscious return to a primitive Benedictine spirit, according to Brother Philip, is marked at Christ in the Desert by an emphasis on communal prayer and on preserving the solitude of the monks for their private prayer. "As you know, 'pray and work' is the principal injunction of St. Benedict to the monk," Brother Philip informs me. "Our work here is in order to support ourselves and to provide a place for those who wish to spend some time at the monastery. Our prayer is the Divine Office and the Eucharist in common, and the private prayer engaged in by each monk: this can be the repetition of the Jesus Prayer, 'lectio divina," which is the prayerful reading of Scriptures or spiritual works, contemplative prayer—this all fits in with the Benedictine tradition.

"Even when we take our meals is based upon the *Rule*. During Lent, we have one meal each day at 4:50 P.M. From Easter to Pentecost, we have one meal at noon and one at 6 P.M. At all other times, we have one meal at 3 P.M. This comes from our belief in the divinely inspired wisdom of St. Benedict, and results in our following the prescriptions of his *Rule*."

Since this is Sunday, there is no work schedule at Christ in the Desert. Brother Philip and I leave the monastic library shortly after 9 A.M. to walk to the church for the chanting of Tierce.

I sit on the bank of the Chama River after Tierce, near a stone building that had been built for those monks who wish to spend some time in total solitude. I gaze at the mesas and wonder about the effect of this community on the life of the Catholic Church in today's society. Can the quiet life of these five monks in this remote spot have any significance? What do their lives mean to a world that puts a premium on such different values? Is there a message in their eating one meatless meal each day? Is there some significance in their eschewing going out to parishes and preaching sermons; in their not setting up a school for the poor Indians in the Rio Arruba country, staffing a hospital, or performing some other aspect of the active apostolate? Are these men merely being self-indulgent in their escape from the world?

The flowing river brings to my mind some words of Thomas Merton, in *Disputed Questions*, with regard to the election of solitude for the monk:

> Withdrawal from other men can be a special form of love for them. It should never be a rejection of man or of his society. But it may well be a quiet and humble refusal to accept the myths and fictions with which social life cannot help but be full—especially today. To despair of the illusions and facades which man builds around himself is certainly not to despair of man. On the contrary, it may be a sign of love and of hope. For when we love someone, we refuse to tolerate what destroys and maims his personality. If we love mankind, can we blind ourselves to man's predicament? You will say: we must do something about his predicament. But there are some whose vocation it is to realize that they, at least, cannot help in any overt social way. Their contribution is a mute witness, a secret and even invisible expression of love which takes the form of their own option for solitude in preference to the acceptance of social functions. For is not our involvement in fiction, particularly in political and demagogic fiction, an implicit confession that we despair of man and even of God?[1]

1. Merton, *Disputed Questions*, pp. 192-193.

11

Paradigms and Experiments

HOUSE OF THE LORD

I could not hold back my feelings of amazement as I entered the old brick building in Memphis, Tennessee, that I could still remember having visited with my mother when I was five years old. It was then a convent of the Poor Clares, a cloistered order of nuns; and the nun to whom we spoke (and who gave me a vial of holy water) we did not see: she was screened behind a grille.

The Poor Clares are now housed next door in a modern building, and their former convent has become the headquarters for a community called the House of the Lord.

The House of the Lord had its beginnings in the struggles of a nun, Sister Diane Myers, with her vocation in the late 1960s, and with her seeking spiritual counsel from a remarkable priest, Father David Knight. Another nun, Sister Lucy Vinturella, also struggling with her vocation, sought Father Knight's help; and the Jesuit theologian and spiritual guide spoke to them of new and more radical spiritual dimensions. Out of these spiritual conferences came a decision to form a religious community.

"We prayed," says Father Knight, "and the Holy Spirit led us step by step."

The trio had met in Louisiana, where Father Knight had been a pastor and Sister Diane and Sister Lucy were engaged in the work assigned to them by their respective religious orders. The two women left their orders in 1972 to form the House of Prayer community in Memphis, Tennessee, the following year.

Perhaps the best description of the House of the Lord is contained in an article by Father Knight that appeared in *Homiletic and Pastoral Review* (June, 1973). The article is entitled "Something Is Missing in the Church," and in it Father Knight writes that a Christian requires:

1. A personal experience of grace; being "touched" by Christ in some way;
2. a community of people who have had this same experience, with whom to pray and express one's faith;
3. ongoing instruction in the spiritual life, in the way to keep growing in one's life in response to Christ.

He goes on to propose the establishment of "centers of spirituality," which would provide:

1. opportunities for an initial, deep experience of God and the grace of Jesus Christ;
2. the possibility of gathering weekly, or even more frequently, with a community of persons who have had a personal experience of grace and who wish to maintain and foster it;
3. continuing personal direction and instruction in the life of grace, its principles of growth, its dangers of illusion, its charted difficulties and the ways discovered thus far to overcome them.

It is the fulfillment of this proposal of "centers of spirituality" that the House of the Lord seeks.

"We were established in Memphis by Bishop Dozier," says Father Knight, "to be two things: a 'house of prayer' for the diocese, and a residence for the permanent community of religious whose own lifestyle sets the tone of the house."

By "house of prayer" is meant a place where people can come to pray, sharing the life of the community in an environment that fosters prayer. "As a 'house of prayer' we differ essentially from a retreat house in this," Father Knight continues, "that guests are integrated into the life of the community during their stay with us, and are helped by the lifestyle of the community to find what they are seeking. Guests share the food, conveniences or inconveniences, and the general living conditions of the community, and are free to participate in all communal prayer and liturgies. Some guests come for a few days of private prayer, spent either in solitude or in participating in the life of the community. Some come for a private retreat and occasionally to make an individually directed retreat. Others come for a longer period—a week, a month. Several stay for as long as a year, during which time they are engaged in a program of prayer, work, and study designed to provide a basic Christian formation."

An abandoned chapel belonging to a community of Poor Clares now serves the same function for the innovative House of the Lord community.

The clanging of a bell is heard in the distance. Father Knight looks at his watch. It is noon—time for midday prayer. We walk together through the labyrinthian corridors of the old convent to the chapel; and here we take our places sitting cross-legged on mats. Each of the dozen persons in the room has a copy of *Daily Prayer for Christians*—a shortened version of the breviary—and the prayers are read from it, alternating between those sitting on one side of the room and those on the other.

Lunch follows prayers; and after we have eaten, I go with Father Knight back to his book-filled office.

"What is it, Father, that distinguishes the House of the Lord from other religious communities of the Church?" I ask.

"This is going to sound more harsh than I intend it to be," he responds without hesitation, "but I don't think that the orders are living their vows of poverty, chastity, and obedience."

The vision of the popular historical view of medieval and Renaissance monasteries and convents indulging in all sorts of excesses comes to me, and I look at Father Knight somewhat open-mouthed.

He notices my surprise and hastens to comment on his startling revelation. "It's not that I think that those who are in religious orders today are rich, not chaste, or disobedient to their superiors; but I don't think most of them are living the Gospels or have an intimate relationship with Jesus Christ. I believe that this is what the nuns who have left their orders to form the House of the Lord have felt; and that is why we've made our fundamental rule living the Gospels and the close relationship with Jesus."

This imitation of Christ for the members of the House of the Lord consists of both a life of prayer and of service. Aside from the house in Memphis, the House of the Lord has a community in nearby Paris, Tennessee, where the community lives in a ramshackle farmhouse and engages in a ministry of visiting the sick, helping the poor, counseling those who are emotionally distressed, and teaching the fundamentals of Christian doctrine to children.

In both Memphis and Paris, even with this active ministry, someone is always left at the house. "We take seriously the idea that we are a 'center of spirituality,' " says Father Knight, "and we believe that someone should always be available for anyone who wishes to come here for any reason."

I have an appointment to speak with Sister Lucy, so I leave Father Knight's study, threading my way down the corridors to the library, where Sister Lucy is waiting.

Short, dark-haired, and with a warm smile, Sister Lucy Vinturella was born in New Orleans in a conventionally pious Italian-American family. She entered the Sisters of St. Joseph after high school, and received her nursing degree while she was in spiritual training.

"It was in the 1960s," Sister Lucy recalls, "and a transitional period in the life of the Church. God had become very abstract for me. I was out to see how modern I could get the order. We wore secular clothes, made collective decisions, and became involved in every social movement that came along. When I was at college, getting my nursing degree, women would come into my room, talk about sex with their boyfriends, problems with birth control, and so forth; and I would just listen—afraid to give witness. I'm still ashamed of that.

"Later, when I was living in our professed house, things got worse. The community was split in two: between those who wanted to live a traditional life and those who wanted a radically modern life. I was among the latter, and I never stopped criticizing those who didn't agree with me."

Sister Lucy discusses how miserable she had become in this environment—until she met Father Knight, who became her spiritual director and taught her to pray.

"Community life became better after that; but I found life too comfortable," she says.

Father Knight told Sister Lucy at this point about Sister Diane's experiment with a new community nearby; and Sister Lucy went to spend some time there before making a decision to join this new community.

"While I was still in my previous order," she tells me, "I had met a French Canadian nun whom I thought terribly old-fashioned. She wore her order's traditional habit, and she talked about her 'passionate love for Jesus Christ.' I didn't like her. And now I've come to realize that she knew what one's life was really all about: a personal love and a following of Jesus Christ."

Sister Diane Myers, who is considered to be the founder of the House of the Lord, joins us. Wearing a brown robe—or habit—without a veil, Sister Diane talks about her life. Born in Erie, Pennsylvania, she worked for a year after she graduated from high school, and then entered the Sisters of the Blessed Sacrament, whose apostolate is to blacks and Indians in the United States.

"I was teaching," says Sister Diane, "and enjoyed what I was doing. But I felt that I was being drawn to a different lifestyle. I made a summer-long retreat directed by Father Knight. I got permission from my superiors for an extension, and lived in a house, praying and discerning what God wanted me to do. I was joined by Sister Lucy and by a couple of other nuns. Together we committed to a way of life to which we felt God was calling us. Father Knight agreed to be our spiritual director; and in 1973 we established ourselves in Memphis."

The growth of the House of the Lord community, both Sister Diane and Sister Lucy tell me, has not been great. There are six members of the community and two others who are committed to spending a year there. It is only after a year of spirituality spent in the community (not geared towards the religious life) that a person is considered a candidate for the community. A minimum of one year and a maximum of three years of spiritual training follow before temporary vows can be taken.

At this time, the sisters tell me, the community is composed entirely of women who have been nuns in other orders. We are still praying to discern whether we should be a mixed community of men and women," Sister Lucy says.

A bell calls us to evening prayer—and then to supper. Between supper and night prayer at 8:30 P.M., I spend time talking with Father Knight. I am eager to discover whether the House of the Lord is a new expression of spirituality for nuns discontented in their former communities, or whether it represents a new movement in the Catholic Church, reflective of Father Knight's own call for "centers of spirituality."

"It's difficult to know what the future holds," says Father Knight, "but I do know that this is what the Lord wants for us. The community tries to live in a way that makes God visible and real. Jesus, the Pearl of Great Price, is truly risen—alive and living among us—loving and caring for us, wanting to lead us to the fullness of life which is found in Him. We want to live in a way that does not make sense unless the reality of Jesus Christ is the central truth of our lives. Therefore, living conditions are deliberately poor. Prayer, both personal and communal, is an explicit part of the day. At atmosphere of charity, silence, and recollection is cultivated in the house. I believe that this witness is something for which Catholics everywhere desire, and that this movement will grow."

Night prayer does not end the day. At 11:45 P.M., I am awakened by a rap on my door: it is time for midnight prayer. Back to bed—and to what seems an instant of sleep—before rising at 6 A.M. I attend morning prayer, meditation, and mass—after which I eagerly consume several cups of coffee at breakfast.

The members of the community go off to various apostolic duties: Sister Lucy to bring parcels of food and clothing to some destitute families, Sister Diane to teach catechism, and Father Knight to give a talk on meditation.

LINDISFARNE

The rain poured down outside as I sat in a simply furnished, neat study in the former rectory of the former Church of the Holy Communion, at West 20th Street and the Avenue of the Americas in New York City, talking to William Irwin Thompson, founder of a community known as Lindisfarne.

Thompson, an historian who resembles an Irish leprechaun, is wearing a thick pullover swater, cotton denim slacks, and sneakers. His short, reddish beard moves up and down as he talks to me about Lindisfarne; and I find myself having difficulty concentrating on what he is saying, fascinated with the verbal pyrotechnics of this youthful-appearing scholar.

Lindisfarne is difficult to categorize. Thompson's experiment with a self-sufficient community at Fishcove on Long Island was abandoned in late 1977. And now Lindisfarne exists only in Manhattan—in a complex of four buildings that were formerly an Episcopalian church. (The buildings, which Lindisfarne leases at a nominal sum from the Episcopal Diocese of New York, consist of a church, built in 1846, a rectory, built in 1896, a parish hall, and a townhouse.) What had been envisaged as a "new age" monastic community is now a loose community of scholars on a spiritual path—much like the group that had gathered about St. Augustine both in Italy and North Africa.

There were sixteen residing at Lindisfarne when I visited. "Fishcove was too expensive to maintain," Thompson informs me, "so we've moved away from the communal model. Also, we didn't want to become a 'spiritual spa,' which is the only way we could have kept Fishcove open." The group adheres to a schedule which calls for rising at 6 A.M., meditation from 6:30 A.M. to 7:15 A.M., work and study until lunch at noon, work and study in the afternoon until 5:30 P.M., when there is meditation for a half-hour, and dinner at 6 P.M., followed at 7 P.M. by classes, lectures, and study. Most of the residents at Lindisfarne have outside jobs to support themselves: others do staff work at the community or support themselves by writing and teaching.

"Lindisfarne is a contemplative educational community in which daily life is shaped by a program of spiritual practice, scholarship, and communal labor," Thompson tells me in an effort to describe the community. "We have weekly house meetings in which we collectively make decisions on operations; and on Wednesday and Saturday afternoons we all work on the reconstruction and maintenance of the buildings. But, aside from these activities, each person at Lindisfarne pursues his or her own life within the broad goals which characterize Lindisfarne."

On Sundays there is what Thompson calls a "communal Christian service." This service is conducted by each member of the community in rotation. "There is always communion and always reading from the New Testament," Thompson says, "but, aside from these two features, the service differs according to the person conducting it. We conduct these religious services based upon our belief in the clergy of the laity. You can say that our orientation is Catholic, but 'catholic' in two ways: most of us are Catholic in backgrounds and style, but we are also 'catholic' in our belief that other paths are also dispensations of the Holy Spirit."

The universality of Lindisfarne is evident in the lists of its fellows, a group of scholars and spiritual masters who meet once a year in a symposium at Lindisfarne and who rotate in coming to live there for a month, teaching and conducting seminars. Among these fellows are Zentatsu Baker-roshi, abbot at the Zen Center in San Francisco; Gregory Bateson, philosopher; Stewart Brand, compiler of the *Whole Earth Catalogue* and editor of the *Co-Evolution Quarterly*; architect Paolo Soleri; and Brother David Steindl-Rast.

"In establishing a teaching center in New York City," Thompson continues, "we are attempting to create a place where individuals can come together in an association dedicated to the resacralization of world culture."

Admission to Lindisfarne is upon application. If the application is accepted, a prospective member of the community lives at Lindisfarne for a month's probationary period. If, at the end of this time, a mutually satisfactory relationship has been established, he or she is accepted as a participating member of the community.

Thompson is hard-headed and realistic about those who wish to become members of spiritual communities. "Most persons joining spiritual communities today do so because of unresolved parental problems," he says. "The spiritual awakening that has become such a factor in this country is both a movement and a fad. That is why we're selective here about the persons who join us. We don't want to run a baby-sitting service for men and women whose emotional instability leads them to seek answers in a spiritual community. And, unlike a lot of communities, where most of the members are in their twenties, those at Lindisfarne tend to be in their thirties. I think it's difficult for people in their twenties to get the concept of contemplative scholarship. They've spent most of their lives in school, and they're academically 'burned out.' When you're in your thirties, this idea of contemplative scholarship becomes more appealing, more capable of being integrated into one's life."

The range of courses at Lindisfarne for the 1978−79 academic year gives an indication of the community's orientation: Sanskrit (one of a revolving number of courses in sacred languages), mythology and the evolution of culture, the Western esoteric tradition, the biology of knowledge, William Blake, sacred architecture, the Kabbala, and the archetype of the feminine in myth and fairy tale.

These are not exactly studies to prepare someone for success in the technological society of the contemporary United States. Thompson, however, believes that this technological society has reached its apex and that new approaches to living are needed. To this end, Thompson applies the term "the resacralization of world culture"—the goal of Lindisfarne.

Thompson believes that Lindisfarne can provide a community for individuals to lead lives towards this "resacralization," as well as a leaven for the country as a whole. The scholars who are affiliated with Lindisfarne read like a Who's Who in Transforming the World. Aside from the fellows mentioned above, those who have been involved with Lindisfarne include Fritjof Capra, author of

The Tao of Physics, poets Alan Ginsberg and Gary Snyder, and the late E. F. Schumacher, author of *Small Is Beautiful* (Harper & Row, 1973).

"This resident community is not yet a fully realized model of planetary culture," says Thompson. "It is a microcosm of a world struggling with making a living, learning to live with a fragile environment, achieving personal integration, and finding trust and love. It is seen as a workshop and forum in which the ideas of planetary thinkers are argued, tested, integrated, and articulated, and through which they are made available to a wider public."

Thompson sees Lindisfarne as modeled on the Benedictine ideal of prayer and work within the context of community life. And although the resident members of Lindisfarne follow different religious paths and the community is receptive to Buddhist and Hindu religious concepts, Thompson adheres to the broad religious concepts of Christianity. "However," he states, "we must rediscover the church of John as opposed to that of Peter."

When I ask Thompson how Lindisfarne supports itself, he responds that the pledges of members ($360.00 annually), fees, and foundation grants keep the community going. Then he enunciates Lindisfarne's philosophy of money. "All of us who have been raised in an industrial civilization have been brought up with certain collective neuroses concerning money," he states. "Some people feel that money is the ultimate value; others feel that money is evil and that truly spiritual people should have nothing to do with it. Lindisfarne accepts the fact that it lives in a society in which money exists, and it neither seeks to store it up nor to cast it away. Although donations of labor are critically important, the ability of the community to use that labor requires enough money to provide the worker with tools, utilities, and materials. Therefore, membership fees are the foundation of Lindisfarne's existence in the city. In establishing a program of lectures, seminars, concerts, poetry readings, exhibitions, meditational retreats, and festivals, Lindisfarne is providing a cultural service for individuals in the city; individuals who become receptive to that service establish a karmic obligation to support the services they use. The awareness of this responsibility is the first and most basic practice of the community's sadhana [spiritual discipline] of mindfulness and self-observation."

Somewhere in the former rectory a bell rings: it is time for evening meditation. Thompson and I walk to the front door together. From various rooms in the building men and women emerge, momentarily leaving their studies to spend a half-hour meditating.

It is still raining as I depart from Lindisfarne. As I look back at the handsome complex of Gothic ecclesiastical buildings, I cannot help wondering whether this community, so reminiscent of those that centered about Pythagoras or those that existed in Renaissance Italy, will truly "resacralize" our society, sending missionaries forth as did the monastery of Lindisfarne during the early Middle Ages, or whether its efforts will be inwardly directed and husbanded for the exclusive use of latter-day gnostics.

BENEDICTINE GRANGE

My taxi drove slowly through the snow-covered landscape of southern Connecticut down a long country lane. Where the road ends, a two-story house—modern, but architecturally akin to an eighteenth- or nineteenth-century New England farmhouse—stands on a knoll overlooking a valley of silvery trees.

Three men come out of the house to greet me and help me carry my things indoors. Soon I come to feel at home with the members of this small monastic group.

Gregory Hauck, the youngest, smiles a greeting as we sit down by the kitchen table. His radiant, exquisitely chiseled face reminds me of a youth in one of Botticelli's paintings.

Father John Giuliani offers me a cup of steaming tea. His handsome face with its short dark beard looks intense, yet compassionate. He wears a black turtleneck sweater and blue jeans. His long fingers lightly hold the teacup. El Greco would have enjoyed these hands.

Brother David Steindl-Rast joins us. He is a man of medium height, with close-cropped salt-and-pepper hair, and a short beard highlighting his austere features. A growing number of spiritual leaders are looking to this Benedictine monk to continue the vision of Thomas Merton, his brother monk and friend, who died a decade ago.

Having made me welcome, the brothers invite me to look

around by myself. At first sight this monastic residence differs little from an ordinary house. And yet a spirit of prayerfulness and of simple beauty is present everywhere. I sense also a quiet joy of living. The kitchen window next to the dining area is crowded with parsley, rosemary, and other herbs growing in pots and planters. The large living room and the two smaller rooms downstairs, one serving as library, are sparsely furnished. Yet, it is obvious that each thing has been given its place with care and with an eye for beauty. Upstairs the original rooms have been subdivided to provide four small bedrooms. There is a bathroom on each floor. The walls are whitewashed throughout the house in pleasant contrast to the woodwork that is left natural. Winter light falls through the windows and I look out on a tree-filled valley below the rock ledge on which this house is built.

Walking outside along an old stone wall that loses itself in the woods I am surprised how still it is here. Only a little over an hour's drive from New York City, these seven acres of land bordering on large tracts of forest are truly a secluded spot. Hidden by dense evergreens lies a separate cottage, where a two-car garage has been converted into a rustic chapel. On Sundays, so many come here for the liturgy that this space is already much too small. During the week, however, the Brothers pray together in their living room.

Dusk is just falling outside as I return to the warm house. I smell wood smoke. Logs are crackling. Above the fireplace an icon of Mary with the Christ Child shines in the light of candles. We stand in front of it for evensong.

The same candle light brightens the supper table as we move into the kitchen after prayer. During the meal I ask John, Gregory, and David why their monastic community is called "Grange." "A grange," they explain, "used to be an outlying farm belonging to a monastery. Only a small group of monks would live there, close to the earth, with greater flexibility of lifestyle, with more solitude, but also with an intimacy of personal relationships not possible in larger establishments. These elements are important to us, too," the brothers say.

Having felt a distinctly monastic atmosphere here, without being able to pinpoint conventional monastic features that would account for my feeling—no gothic arches, no cowls and hoods, no Gregorian chant—I inquire about the specifically monastic character of the Benedictine Grange.

"There is nothing wrong with arches and hoods and chant," Brother David answers. "Personally, these things are very much

Brother David Steindl-Rast spends his mornings writing at Benedictine Grange.

to my taste. But there is one decisive feature that makes an environment monastic: mindfulness. In fact, that's what a monastery is anywhere in the world, a place designed to foster mindfulness."

"Mindfulness in all its dimensions," Father John adds, "from the way we treat our garden tools, to responsible awareness of global issues, the arms race, exploitation, hunger." Gregory tells of Good

Shepherd House of Hospitality in nearby Norwalk, an outreach of the Grange, of which he is in charge. Forty and more hungry people come there every day for a warm meal and for assurance that someone is mindful of them and cares. "Of course," he adds, "what we receive is so much more than what we can give. Often I'm overwhelmed by gratefulness."

Gratefulness, my three hosts agree, is inseparable from mindfulness. The problem, as they see it, is that our affluent society conditions us to take more and more things for granted. But what we take for granted does not make us happy; it means nothing to us. Thus, as gratefulness deteriorates, happiness is lost, and the meaning of life is lost. They see their monastic foundation as a school for grateful living. More and more people experience today a need to spend time in such a place. The brothers hope to be able to accommodate such people at the Grange before too long. But even now, there are scores of non-residents who belong to what one might call the extended community. Some come almost daily for worship; many more on Sundays, sometimes from great distances. There are also special *ora et labora* days when friends join the residents at the Benedictine Grange for prayer and special work projects.

"One of the important re-discoveries within monastic renewal today," Brother David explains, "is that monastic community allows for many different shades and degrees of commitment and belonging. It isn't either in or out, as we used to think—here the monks, there the outside world. There is an increasing need in our mobile society for stable centers to which people can periodically return as to their spiritual home. It seems that the Benedictine Grange is already beginning to fulfill this function for a growing number of people."

I ask how the community functions economically, and the brothers tell me that they figure out how much it costs per day to run the place and divide that amount by the number of residents. Each is responsible for his share, which he might earn through work compatible with life at the Grange or during periods when he is not in residence there. "It's just a different model," as they put it, "for cultivating detachment and responsibility, two important elements of monastic tradition."

We have meanwhile gotten up from our meal. Gregory washes dishes while I wipe. Born in South Bend, Indiana, in 1957, and baptized an Episcopalian, Gregory grew up with little interest in religion, at least in the forms in which he had come to know it. In his heart he seems to have been a deeply religious seeker, like so many of his generation. What turned him on was religious experience, not doctrines or moral precepts. Friends prayed together; he joined them and so found a focus for his religous longing.

Then a friend took him along to Mass. The way Father John celebrated that liturgy was also a religious experience for Gregory. Eventually he took instructions and became a Roman Catholic. But again, like others of his alienated generation, Gregory felt a deep need for community on many different levels. What he is finding at the Benedictine Grange is a community that offers spiritual support, personal warmth, and social outreach. He is in charge of the garden and marvels at the goodness of the soil that yields food for the table at the Grange and at Good Shepherd House of Hospitality. Gregory's gentle smile conveys the joy of sharing.

The next morning I was to experience the source of that joy. "Life at the Benedictine Grange is centered in the Eucharist and overflows into hospitality and grateful living," I had read in a one-sheet folder about the community. Now, quite a while before sunrise, still wiping the sleep out of my eyes, I find myself in the living room again, where a bell has called us together for the celebration of the Eucharist. We are seated in a circle on a Navajo rug; bread, wine, and Gospel book in the center. Each of us takes a turn in reading the day's selection from Scripture. "Where two or three are gathered in My Name . . ." Then Father John breaks the bread. He passes the earthenware chalice that has a sandy roughness to the touch. Dawn breaks as we sit in silence.

Later, I ask Father John how he happened to become a member of the Benedictine Grange. The handsome priest, whose youthful looks belie his forty-five years, was born in Greenwich, Connecticut, and studied to become an artist. "While at Pratt Institute, I happened upon the writings of Augustine and Thomas Merton," he tells me. "They indirectly influenced my decision to study for the priesthood. What really inspired me was the monastic ideal, but that seemed practically out of reach from where I was at the time."

John entered St. John's Seminary in Boston, was ordained for the Diocese of Bridgeport, and spent most of his time as a priest teaching. Fortunately, his bishop was sensitive to Father John's real calling. He encouraged him to search for a life-style that would allow his personal vocation to unfold, realizing that in this way he would also be of most benefit to the diocese. "At the time Brother David decided to leave Maine, Gregory and I," Father John tells me, "had already been living in community. We were sharing the work of hospitality at Good Shepherd House. It was then that Brother David's and our monastic interests converged and together we founded the Benedictine Grange here."

This leads me to inquire about the venture in Maine. It was there that, for three years, Brother David conducted a monastic experiment before moving here. This spare, intense monk born in the mid-1920's in Austria, is today considered one of the most innovative spiritual leaders in the United States. With degrees in art and anthropology and a doctoral degree in psychology from the University of Vienna, David came to the United States in 1952 and soon joined Mount Saviour Monastery, founded shortly before. "I am grateful to my brothers at Mt. Saviour," he says, "for backing me up in a task that seems vital today: to help channel the wisdom of tradition into forms that meet the needs and opportunities of our time. And I am grateful to my brothers here at the Grange. Since I must travel and lecture some three or four months every year, they hide me here the rest of the time as a sort of hermit in residence."

"In Maine," he tells me, "the emphasis was on the hermit's life. That is one pole of the current monastic renewal, community life is another. For some the need to experience intensive sharing is more pressing, for others the need for a time of radical solitude. Most of us need both, but rhythm and intensity have to be adjusted to personal requirements. What we are trying to build up here at the Grange is a central position, as it were. At its core, a closely knit community, but with room for those whose needs differ. They should also feel at home here. In time we hope to combine hermitages up in Maine with our central base here, just as we hope to extend ourselves further in the opposite direction through intensified service of those in need. But for the time being our energy must be devoted to strengthening this central foothold."

It is time for work now, deskwork or work outdoors. Since the house is heated mostly by woodstoves, there plenty of work outside, even now in the winter, gathering, cutting, and splitting firewood. Shafts of sunlight pour into the study where letters, books, and notes are piled on the large desk. Outside, the snow-covered ground glistens in the sunlight, and the silvery oak, birch, maple and beech trees silently wait for Spring. I walk through the snow to a rock ledge and look back on this monastic dwelling. Thin smoke is rising from the chimney. "The word 'grange'—*granarium* in Latin—originally meant a grain bin," one of the brothers had told me, "a place where the seed grain is stored through the winter." I like to think of this Benedictine Grange as a place where seed is kept alive for a new sowing. My thoughts fly ahead to visions of a new monastic spring.

A Bibliographical Essay

I N such a book as *Living Together Alone*, in which a description and interpretation of the new importance of the revived spiritual community deals with as yet unexplored issues, a suggested bibliography must of necessity be a limited *vade mecum* for the person who wishes to study further the field of the "new monasticism." Such it is: a vehicle for the pilgrim to continue his or her search into the roots and contemporary experience of contemporary U.S. spiritual communities.

There are numerous books on Christian monasticism. Key to the understanding of Western monasticism is the *Rule* of St. Benedict, which is available in numerous editions. David Knowles' *Christian Monasticism* (London: World University Library, 1969) is a useful survey of the field by this authority on the history of Western monasticism. Christian monasticism in the context of Christian spirituality is treated most notably by Louis Bouyer in *The Spirituality of the New Testament and the Fathers* (New York: Descler, 1963) and by the Jesuits Thomas M. Gannon and George W. Traub in *The Desert and the City; an interpretation of the history of Christian spirituality* (New York: Macmillan & Co., 1969).

The increasing literature on the Eastern religious impact in the United States is best represented by Jacob Needleman's pioneering work *The New Religions* (New York: Doubleday & Co., 1970), by Harvey Cox's personal essay *Turning East* (New York: Simon & Schuster, 1977), and by Harrison Pipe, Jr.'s *The Road East:*

America's New Discovery of Eastern Wisdom (Boston: Beacon Press, 1974).

There is also an increasing amount of literature providing some synthesis between Eastern metaphysics and religious thought and Christian doctrine and spirituality. The works of Dom Aelred Graham and the writings of Thomas Merton provide early statements on this topic. William Johnston's *Christian Zen* (New York: Harper & Row, 1974) and J.-M. Dechanet's *Christian Yoga* (New York: Harper & Row, 1972) are important contributions.

The Catholic charismatic movement has developed an extensive literature during the past decade. Most of the writings on Catholic pentecostalism are by charismatics themselves. The foremost theologian writing about the charismatic movement from a theological perspective is Donald L. Gelpi, S.J., of the Graduate Theological Union in Berkeley, California. Among his many works, *Pentecostalism, A Theological Viewpoint* (New York: Paulist Press, 1971) is a valuable source despite its having been written shortly after the Catholic charismatic movement began.

Both Chogyam Trungpa and Baba Muktananda have written extensively. Trungpa's *Born in Tibet* (Hammondsworth, Middlesex, England: Penguin Books, 1971), *Cutting Through Spiritual Materialism* (Berkeley: Shambala, 1973) and *The Myth of Freedom and the Way of Meditation* (Berkeley and London: Shambala, 1976) provide both autobiographical and metaphysical insights into this growing Buddhist movement.

The S.Y.D.A. Foundation, which publishes the books of Baba Muktananda, has a large publishing program. Muktananda's *Play of Consciousness* (San Francisco: Harper & Row, 1979) and the volumes of *Satsang with Baba*, which are composed of questions and answers between Muktananda and his devotees, are excellent starting points for understanding the Hinduism of Muktananda.

There are numerous books on the history and thought of Buddhism. The popular books of Alan Watts, those of Christmas Humphreys, and the scholarly writings of D. T. Suzuki are all readily available. The scholarly German Jesuit Heinrich Dumoulin's *A History of Zen Buddhism*, translated by Paul Peachey (New York: Pantheon Books, 1963) is excellent.

For Hinduism, Thomas J. Hopkins' *The Hindu Religious Tradition* (Encino, California: Dickenson Publishing Company, 1971) is a good place to begin.